**KT-376-087**

# GROWING
## Cacti & Succulents

GROWING
# Cacti
# & Succulents

## by Douglas Bartrum

*Illustrations by Sandra Grantham*
*photographs by Harry Smith*

**JOHN BARTHOLOMEW & SON LTD**
Edinburgh

© Douglas Bartrum 1973
First published 1974
by John Bartholomew and Son Ltd.
12 Duncan Street, Edinburgh EH9 1TA
Also at 216 High Street, Bromley BR1 1PW
ISBN 0 85152 938 0

Designed by Youé and Spooner Ltd

Filmset by Filmtype Services Limited, Scarborough
Printed by Morrison and Gibb Ltd.
Edinburgh and London

# Contents

## LIST OF COLOUR PLATES

# Preface

People who are especially interested in growing Cacti are usually town and city-dwellers, those without gardens or with only a small yard. They may succeed with one or two hardy Succulents outside (all they have room for), such as the popular *Sedum spectabile* (often called the Ice Plant), a largish herbaceous plant with juicy green leaves and big flat pink-red flower-heads; but Cacti give them more pleasure, for these are permanent and do not die down and disappear for months as do many of the hardy Succulents. People with gardens often grow Cacti indoors for a winter display and choose the best of the hardy Succulents for outside.

There is a great variety of plants to choose from – for greenhouses, glass lean-to's, or an ordinary living-room, where perforce most of us grow them.

This book has been written to show readers how to grow Cacti and Succulents indoors and outside.

Part 1 deals with Cacti, nearly all of which are tender and must be housed.

Part 2 describes most of the favourite Succulents, both the tender and the hardy kinds.

The vast majority of the plants can be obtained from nurseries and florists. But I have included some which are more difficult to get but are from time to time offered for sale.

Popular names are given, when these exist – most readers like them – and also the meaning, when known, of the specific epithets.

D.B.

# Chapter One
# General Remarks

Not *all* cacti are hot-house plants or native only to America: for instance, the Prickly Pear – *Opuntia* – can be seen growing outside in warm, sheltered spots in the south of England, a country which is not normally favoured with hot weather!

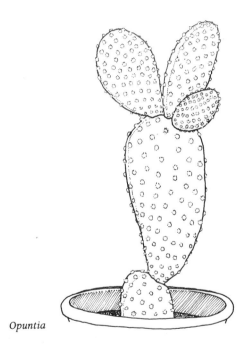

*Opuntia*

The family *Cactaceae* comprises over a hundred different genera and *Opuntia* is one of the best known. *Cactus* is a genus, besides being the common name of all cacti. (It is worthwhile mentioning in passing that the plural *cacti* is preferable to *cactuses*, which one often hears).

The reader probably doesn't know *Ariocarpus, Bartschella, Cochemiea, Dolichothele*, to name only four genera of cacti. I once asked a gardener to name off-hand a few genera, but the only one he could think of was *Cereus*, several species of which he grew. But he knew *Agave, Aloe, Euphorbia, Sedum, Sempervivum,* succulents belonging to different families. The first two I have often heard called cacti; they have fat, fleshy, leaves such as one associates with cacti, though the so-called 'leaves' of these plants are really swollen fleshy stems, not leaves. In most genera leaves are absent or are reduced to scales and scarcely noticeable.[1]

Let us first look at the cactus family. Although mostly grown indoors and in pots of special soil, prepared by the nurseries who sell them to the shops – where we buy them – cacti may be put outside in the open garden all through the hot summer months and will benefit from it – left in their pots, of course, unless you have a spot which is always warm and sheltered, and can leave the suitable ones (*Opuntia*) outside permanently.

*Opuntia vulgaris* (*O. Rafinesqui*: a synonym) is a reasonably-hardy species and has been grown successfully in warm localities. We might use it to illustrate some of the different characters of cacti. It is common in South America.[2]

First, the generic name *Opuntia* (accent on the second syllable): it seems to have been derived from *Opus*, a town in the vicinity of Phocis, a province of ancient Greece – apparently cactus-like plants grew there.[3]

The specific epithet *vulgaris* means common. This species has been naturalised in many parts of the globe.

The oblongish joints (flat juicy stems – narrower at the base) have *areoles* with short wool; *glochids*, brown in colour; and spines on the marginal *areoles*.

The *areole* is an organ peculiar to cacti – the word is from the Latin, meaning a tiny space or area. *Areoles* bear spines, felt, bristles, hairs.

*Glochids* are short barbed bristles, stiff and penetrating and become easily attached to the skin. They are usually grouped in bundles in the upper part of the *areoles*.

*Opuntia* flowers are cup- or saucer-shaped and come singly at the top of the joints or sections.

The fruits are pear-shaped (hence the popular name PRICKLY PEAR) and often edible.

The leaves are tiny and soon fall.

A few more general remarks. There are about 2000 different species of cacti and no other plants have so many diversities of shapes and forms. In size cacti range from exiguous, stone-like plants to the giant

[1]Only a few cacti form true leaves: *Pereskia*, for instance. See page 11. See also some of the Opuntias, e.g. *O. subulata*, page 81.
[2]It is now described by many botanists under *O. opuntia*.
[3]See page 87, Chapter 3.

*Cereus* of Arizona, particularly the 40-foot one called Sahuaro by the Red Indians. And they can be round – ball-like; flat, pad-like; tall, columnar; or have pendent stems – these being ideal plants for hanging pots or baskets. Their beauty is often enhanced by gorgeous flowers – some scented, such as those of certain *Echinopsis*; and also by their coloured spines, hairs, fruits. Wonderfully decorative most of them and ideal for growing in our warm rooms where they can get all the sun possible.

The thorns and spines serve the purpose of protecting the plants from browsing animals. High up in the Andes, for instance, llamas munch away at the sparse vegetation but avoid getting too near the cacti that grow there.

Although usually untouched and unharmed by wild animals, they are not safe from the depredations of birds and insects. Birds carry seeds for miles and drop them in places where they germinate and produce new plants; even minute pieces of stems, which birds peck off, will root in certain places where they are undisturbed. So hundreds of birds will produce hundreds of thousands of new plants; so many that they quickly become pests on land that has to be cultivated.

Cacti, with their succulent stems and water storage tissues, are able to exist for long periods without any rain. The thick skin, together with the absence of leaves, enables them to thrive; if they had leaves or normal leaves the plants would lose much moisture through transpiration (giving off moisture or water through leaves – see, however, the genus *Pereskia*, which has persistent leaves). When the rain does come, in a torrential downpour, it is quickly absorbed by the widespreading roots; so quickly, in fact, and so much of it is imbibed that occasionally the tissues of some cacti burst. No serious damage is done to the plants, however, and they soon recover.

Indoors, cacti can be well looked after: we can give them all the water they want – at the correct temperature – and keep them in a warm, sunny place.

Before discussing their cultivation, it is perhaps only necessary to add that *all* cacti are perennials: none is an annual.

2

The temperature of the room, greenhouse or conservatory where cacti grow should not fall below 45F (7C).

Most of them need all the sun they can get, but must be protected from long spells of scorching summer heat. I find that the easiest way to protect them is simply to draw the curtains; that is, if you have the plants standing in long rows, say, on a window-sill, and turning the

11

plants round now and again benefits them. Greenhouses or cactus houses are usually provided with suitable blinds.

The next important thing to temperature and sun is moisture. It is pretty obvious that plants grown in containers need more than those in the open ground; they soon use up what there is in the small amount of soil, the roots growing quickly and strongly in a limited space. And a restricted root-run eventually causes the plants to become pot-bound – re-potting is then usually necessary (see below).

It may be necessary to water them daily during hot summers; those that are well matured and fill or almost overlap their pots should be stood in receptacles containing a little water to enable the roots to imbibe – through the porous pot – all they want. (Do not plant cacti in glazed pots or pans.) Rain water should always be used and at the right temperature: never icy water straight from tanks or butts outdoors. If no rain water is available tap water which has stood for some hours in the sun to warm up will be all right: it is best treated with a suitable chemical preparation designed to correct iron deficiency in alkaline soils.

Late evening or early morning, when the sun's rays have less power, is the best time for watering. No stimulants such as liquid manure are necessary. A small watering-can with a tapered spout which carries the water straight on to the soil without splashing the plants is recommended by the experts.

A common question: 'How can I tell when my cacti want watering?' The surface soil is usually pale or dusty-looking. Tap the pot: if you get a ringing sound the soil is too dry.

During the winter or the resting period, drier conditions are required by most cacti; but those in flower or in bud, such as the *Zygocactus* (in bloom at Christmas) need a fair amount of moisture. And those that are still growing and forming buds at this time – the *Epiphyllum*: some bloom in February – must also be watered now and then.

All cacti benefit from an occasional spraying with rain water, especially during hot summer days. An alternative treatment is to stand them outside when the weather is showery. Most growers do this normally throughout the summer months, anyway, bringing them in when the weather turns very wet and dull, or when the plants are about to flower. One likes to watch the flowers blooming indoors.

Cacti should be re-potted only when it is absolutely necessary – I have a Prickly Pear which has been growing in the same pot for five years and is still in a flourishing state. One sign that it really does need re-potting now is the appearance of roots through the drainage hole. I shall re-pot after the soil has been well soaked: the plant should then come out fairly easily. Often, however, it is necessary to break the pot to get a plant out without damaging the roots. Tap it all round with a hammer till it cracks and breaks. If by chance the roots are torn in the process cut the damaged ones across cleanly with a sharp pair of scissors. Let any plants with damaged roots settle down for a period before watering them again. You will need only a slightly larger pot: so usually a cactus growing in a $4\frac{1}{2}$ inch pot will transplant well into the next size – a 6 inch pot (these measurements are of the top inside diameter).

*Epiphyllum*

Adequate drainage material – broken crocks – must be put at the bottom before you add the soil; the correct soils are described along with the plants later on in the book. But most of them will thrive in a mixture of 4 parts of lightish garden loam and one part of equal quantities of sharp sand and brick rubble. A grower of my acquaintance says: 'I always add a quarter-of-an-inch layer of finely-sifted leafmould on top'. A good idea: it helps to keep the soil underneath moist. The best time for re-potting is early spring, just before the plants begin to make new growth.

Propagation of cacti is effected by cuttings, seeds or by grafting. The easiest and quickest way is by offsets, those small pieces, often with roots attached, that grow round the lower part of the main stems. These are simply detached and planted in equal parts of loam and sand. No watering is necessary till the little plants are well established. Offsets must be taken in summer.

Cuttings are small pieces of shoots or stems taken from any part of the plant; suitable small pieces are usually available. With some kinds, however – *Cereus*, for instance – it is necessary to divide the main stem up into smallish portions. The cuttings are left to dry for a time, till they form a corky skin over the cut part; they are then inserted in pots of sandy loam and left to grow. Cuttings must be taken during spring and summer.

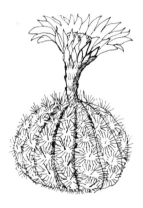

*Notocactus*

The faster-growing cacti are often raised from seeds. Those that take a long time to germinate and to flower are scarcely worth growing from seed. Plant the seeds in sandy loam (or a seed compost) and cover with a pane of glass shaded with a piece of paper. Leave the seedlings till big enough to prick out into boxes; then, when larger, plant them singly in tiny 1-inch pots. Temperature for cactus seeds should be 65–70F.

*Pereskia aculeata*

Special methods are recommended for propagating certain cacti; these are included with the description of the plants.

Some cacti are best grafted on others, especially those that are of comparatively weak growth and liable to decay at the lower part of the stem. It is always advisable to propagate these by grafting them on strong growing stock: *Pereskia aculeata* is one of the cacti frequently used. Amateurs on the whole prefer to increase their plants by offsets (when these are produced), cuttings and seeds.

A collection of cacti

*Astrophytum ornatus,* an easy cactus
to grow in a small pot          17

*Astrophytum myriostigma*, a choice
cactus easily grown indoors

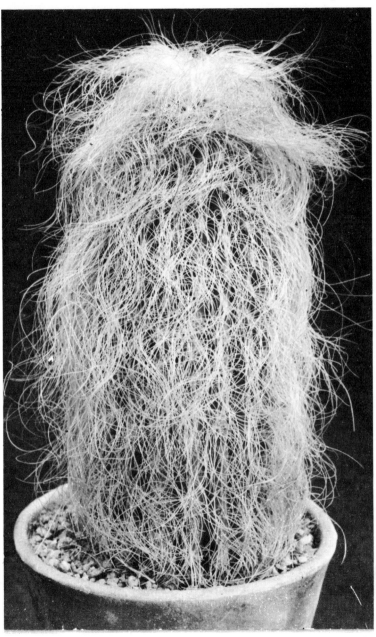

*Cephalocereus senilis*, old-man cactus,
a special favourite with collectors   19

*Cleistocactus strausii,* a choice cactus
from South America  20

*Echinocactus Grusonii*, the Golden Ball cactus which provides sap to drink for travellers in the desert

*Echinopsis eyriesii*, a lovely cactus
which bears large white flowers

*Epiphyllum oxypetalum*

23

*Ferocactus stainesii*

*Mammilaria erythrosperma*

*Oreocereus Celsianus*

*Rebutia xanthocarpus*

*Zygocactus truncatus,* which blooms
at Christmas, is one of the most **28**
popular of all cacti

*Opuntia basilaris*

*Opuntia microdasys*

*Lobivia carminantha*

# Chapter Two
# Some Popular Cacti.
# The Cereeae Group

Anybody who has studied botany will be aware of the confusion that exists in plant nomenclature. However, the average gardener isn't much interested in names – he is principally concerned with cultivation. Names are important only in so far as they enable him to get hold of the right plant for his garden or his greenhouse. A little incident illustrating the confusion we still come across: A customer once asked a florist for a specimen of the favourite Rat's Tail Cactus and got a good plant in flower. When he reached home he discovered it was labelled *Aporocactus flagelliformis,* and that a neighbour who had an older, bigger, plant had his labelled *Cereus flagelliformis*. A catalogue he consulted gave the first name but did not include the second (*Cereus*) – not even as a synonym (which is sometimes done). A book on cacti published in 1930, which he had read, called the plant *Cereus flagelliformis*.

Plant nomenclature is a dreary subject and the average reader finds it enormously boring. The important thing is to know how to grow a plant successfully.

*Aporocactus* belong to the CEREEAE tribe or group, which is by far the largest of the three tribes into which cacti are divided. I have chosen some of the most popular plants; they are all obtainable from nurseries and florists and I shall describe first the Rat's Tail Cactus, known to everybody surely, and among the easiest to grow.

First the two generic names – *Cereus* (to which genus it formerly belonged): the word is from the Latin *cera*, meaning wax or torch; the old popular name of the Cerei was Torch Thistle, adopted by early botanists probably because the tall columnar ones resembled torches and were prickly. *Aporocactus,* the genus under which the plant is now described: the word means 'impenetrable cactus' but is in no way descriptive of the plants or of their characters. The specific epithet *flagelliformis* means 'having long thin shaped shoots'.

*Aporocactus flagelliformis* (*Cereus flagelliformis*) comes from Mexico

Plate I *Aporocactus flagelliformis*, the Rat's Tail cactus, an easy cactus to grow

Plate II *Chamaecereus silvestrii*, a favourite cactus with amateurs and easy to grow

Plate III *Notocactus scopa* var. *Can-dida*, with bright lemon-yellow flowers

and Central America and is not known in the wild state. It has slender, soft, hanging stems, ribbed and closely studded with areoles on which are tiny reddish-brown spines. The flowers, which come singly along the stems, are crimson, about 3 inches long and 2 inches across and bloom usually in April; they last several days but seldom more than a week. The plants we get from the shops are mostly grafted on *Selenicereus Macdonaldiae* stock; but this *Aporocactus* does well on its own roots. I like to see it in a basket, with its greyish-green stems hanging over the sides; when in full bloom the crimson trumpet-like flowers stand out well and the whole plant is very decorative. Grow it in a mixture of equal parts of fibrous loam, leafmould and coarse sand. Water liberally in April; give less after the flowering season, and just keep the soil from getting dust-dry during the winter months. The room temperature should not fall below 45F (7C) and the position should always be bright and sunny.

*Aporocactus flagelliformis*

Propagation is by grafting, by seeds in spring (they take a long time to germinate), or by cuttings in summer – pull off smallish pieces, put them on a sunny shelf in a greenhouse to harden the raw cut part and then set them in well-drained pots of sandy soil mixed with crushed brick. Keep this compost only reasonably moist.

There are several other species, none, however, as well known as the Rat's Tail Cactus. Perhaps the loveliest of them is *Aporocactus Mallisonii* (*Cereus nothus*), which most botanists consider a hybrid between *A. flagelliformis* and a species of *Heliocereus*. It is a large-flowered plant (raised in England) with big glowing red flowers, which come in profusion during April.

*Aporocactus mallisonii*

The Christmas Cactus or Crab Cactus is probably as popular as the Rat's Tail; and another is the Old Man Cactus, which has a long upright stem covered with a dense mat of white hair-like bristles.

Both belong to the CEREEAE group and each is described in its place further on in the chapter. The alphabetical arrangement will best help readers to find what cacti they want.

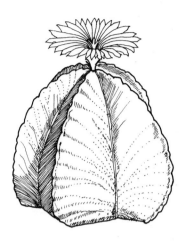

*Astrophytum myriostigma*

*Astrophytum myriostigma* (*Echinocactus myriostigma* is the synonym and the name is still used by some florists). The generic name is derived from the words '*aster*' (star), and *phytos* (plant) and alludes to the shape of the plant. There are four species; none is really like a star – though perhaps the name refers to the five-ribbed shape of some plants. The popular name of our species is more appropriate, viz. Bishop's Cap – the five-ribbed globular forms do somewhat resemble a Bishop's mitre. The specific epithet, like many another, is something of a puzzle: *myrio* (many) and *stigma*; it may refer to the flower.

The areoles, along the crest of each rib, come close together and are woolly but spineless. The natural pale green of the plant is covered completely by minute white star-like scales or hairs. This is one of its great attractions. The flowers arise from areoles on the top or crown, usually after about three years or when the plant measures roughly $2\frac{1}{2}$ inches across. They are from 2 to 3 inches wide, a lovely satiny yellow and bloom in summer.

This is a choice cactus, prized by all collectors, of easy cultivation and, like the other species and varieties, revels in full sun. Keep *Astrophytum* well supplied with water from April to September. They need porous sandy soil, rich in lime, with an admixture of leafmould and old powdered cow manure. They are mostly raised from seeds.

The species is a native of central Mexico and is found on stony hillsides 7500 feet above sea level.

Many varieties are offered by nurseries; among the most desirable is *A. m. var. coahuilensis* (*from Coahuila, Mexico*). This is a favourite with collectors on account of its grey-white colouring (it is densely clothed with whitish scales which give it a curiously attractive velvety appearance) and its richly-scented flowers, yellow with an orange centre. A beautiful cactus.

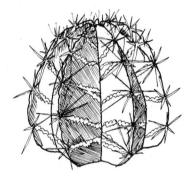

*Astrophytum ornatus*

*A. ornatus* (*showy*) is indeed a showy plant, with its largish, lemon-yellow flowers and 2-inch spines, which are first a sulphur-yellow, then turn brown. The plant body or stem is mostly eight-ribbed and globular and with age grows more cylindrical. Another attraction is the marking of silvery-white scales which come in fairly regular bands all round the stem. The spines on the areoles usually number 5 to 11 and are exceptionally sharp. This cactus is sometimes considered to be a natural hybrid between the above species and an *Echinocactus*. It resembles the former except that the edges or crests of the ribs are sharper and wavy.

The plant is grown like the other; it is one of the easiest and toughest of the popular cacti. It is raised from seed and the seedlings grow quickly. (Like the other species it was formerly called a *Cereus*.)

Two varieties are offered by nurseries; viz. *Var. Mirbelli*, described as 'A lovely form, completely covered with scales of a shining white'. It has very attractive golden-yellow spines. And *Var. glabrescens,* which has white scales here and there and yellow brownish spines.

*Carnegiea gigantea* (*unusually tall*). The genus was named in honour of Andrew Carnegie, the philanthropist. This is the giant columnar cactus, with branching stems, a native of Arizona and Sonora in Mexico. Specimens 40 feet high may be seen growing there in the desert wastes, the plants standing up like strange monuments of some past civilisation.

These giant cacti are described by some writers as trees and are exceptionally slow growers. In their young state they make charming pot plants and prosper well indoors. You may occasionally see specimens grown in specially-prepared beds of soil in conservatories. But no cultivated plants ever bloom. Flowers appear only on old plants in the wild.

This cactus (grey-green in colour) is ribbed; often the ribs are numerous; the areoles are about an inch apart, with dense brown wool; and the spines are brown and grey. The flowers, produced near the top of the plant, are white and about 5 inches long and as much in width. The fruit is a berry with red pulp and much enjoyed by the native Indians. A special cultural hint – as this cactus has roots which spread wide naturally it needs a large-bottomed pan; this is much better than an ordinary flowerpot. It is a slow grower and takes centuries to reach maturity. Seed can be obtained from most cacti nurseries.

Finally, *Carnegiea gigantea* has several synonyms; the one usually quoted is *Cereus gigantea*.

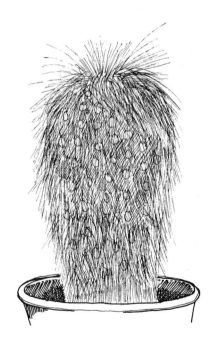

*Cephalocereus senilis*

*Cephalocereus senilis* (*grey-haired, appearing old,* on account of the white hair-like bristles which grow in tufts or tresses on the upper part of old plants). This is the famous Old Man Cactus. A special favourite with collectors. The generic name is from *Kephale,* head and *Cereus* – the plant produces a woolly or hairy head when of flowering size. There is an attractive form called *Var. longiseta,* which has longer hairs and a thicker stem – it seems a little difficult to get at the moment.

*C. senilis* is a native of Mexico, where it is found growing in the fissures of slaty rock and when old and mature is often 45 feet tall. In shape it is columnar, only occasionally branching from the base. The stem is light green at first, then becomes grey with age, and is ribbed. The areoles are large and round, closely set and produce both spines and the characteristic long white hairs.

The flowers appear on plants when they reach the height of about 18 feet; they are nocturnal, 2 inches long and rose-pink in colour. They grow from a woolly, hairy part, called the pseudo-cephalium, near the apex of the plant. This cactus needs a winter temperature round about 50F (10C). Personally, I have never seen any specimens in cultivation more than about 12 inches tall – and these are quite old. Young plants

have longer, whiter, hairs than older ones; occasionally, on imported plants, the hairs are dirty and matted but they are easily washed and cleaned in warmish soapy water. These cacti must be well rinsed before planting them in pots.

There are many other species and varieties but few are offered by florists and nurseries. The synonym of our plant often found on labels is *Pilocereus senilis*.

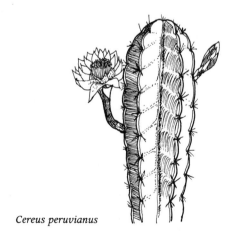

*Cereus peruvianus*

*Cereus peruvianus (Peruvian)*; the plant is not found in Peru, however; it is native to south-eastern Brazil and northern Argentina. The name is therefore a misnomer. In the wild the plant reaches a height of 40 feet or so and is freely branched, the stems sometimes being glaucous. They are deeply ribbed and bear areoles about an inch apart; from these come brownish-coloured spines. The flowers, white within and brownish on the outside, are about 6 inches long, with a thick tube, and they appear only on mature plants.

There are several cristate forms (varieties with a crest or head); the one familiarly known as the Rock Cactus, *Var. monstrosus nana,* a dwarf form, is the best known – at least it is most easily obtainable. Both the type (the species) and the varieties like a soil rich in lime and are quite easy to grow.

*C. jamacaru (syn. C. lividus, C. validus)* is another species easily obtainable from florists and nurseries. One of its attractions is the blue colour of the stems when young. The flowers (greenish-white) and spines are both long in old plants – I have seen spines nearly a foot long – and flowers almost that length. An easy plant to grow in a pot indoors.

*Chamaecereus Silvestrii*

*Chamaecereus Silvestrii* (named in honour of Dr. Philippo Silvestri, the botanist, who discovered the plant in Argentina). The generic name is from *chamai,* on the ground, and *cereus;* meaning the *cereus* that grows along the ground. It is the only species; the synonym is *Cereus Silvestrii.* The stems or branches, which are numerous, are light green, and the shortest are easily detached (and very easily broken off); these quickly take root and form new plants. The stems are ribbed, with closely-set areoles bearing tiny white bristle-like spines. The flowers are magnificent – a glowing orange scarlet and funnel shaped; and they are diurnal (blooming during the day). A favourite little cactus, which needs full sunshine and plenty of water in the growing season. The popular name apparently is the Pea Nut Cactus. There are several varieties; the one most often seen is *Var. lutea* (*yellowish*), with etiolated (yellow) stems. Spray these cacti quite frequently to keep the red spider mite away.[1]

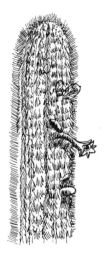

*Cleistocactus Strausii*

*Cleistocactus Strausii* (*cleist,* closed; the flowers are never fully open).[2] This choice cactus is a native of the mountains of Bolivia, South America, where it reaches a height of 4 feet or more. In cultivation it is a much smaller plant and blooms only when well established, usually when it reaches about 3 feet in height. The stems are slender, erect, not more than 2 inches in diameter and have about 25 ribs. (In some species the stems are decumbent; that is, they lie along the ground and are erect at the ends.) The colour, green, is almost hidden by the masses of attractive white hair-like bristles or spines. The flowers come laterally (along the sides of the plant) and are carmine in colour; they contrast beautifully with the white-green colouring of the stems. Altogether a curiously beautiful cactus for collectors. A number of varieties are offered: the one with glassy white bristles is most in demand. The plants usually send up offshoots from the base; and these shoots may be used to increase one's stock. They seldom branch, however, unless they are topped for a similar purpose – or perhaps in the wild by accident.

[1]See Chapter four, page 121.
[2]See Chapter four, page 122.

*Coryphantha clava* (*club-shaped*; referring to the shape of the stem). There are more than 50 different species, all natives of Mexico. According to one specialist they like sun on them all through the year. For my part I have found that *C. clava* does just as well, if not better, in part shade and that it likes some powdered leaf-mould mixed in with the usual sandy, gritty cactus soil.

The plant is furnished with prominent tubercles or warts, conically shaped; and these bear areoles with $\frac{1}{2}$-inch yellow marginal spines and longer central brownish spines. The axils of the tubercles have white wool and reddish glands; the flowers, yellowish within, green on the outside, are large and showy. The synonym is *Mammillaria clava* – *Coryphantha* were formerly described under the genus *Mammillaria* (see page 53).

*Coryphantha clava*

*C. erecta* (*upright*; referring to the stems). It comes from the same part of Mexico (Hidalgo) as other species and both appear to be the most popular of the genus. In cultivation *C. erecta* usually has a single stem but in the wild produces clusters; these stems are about 12 inches long and erect at the ends. The tubercles are small, rounded and conical and the axils very woolly. The spines are yellowish at first, then later become a brownish colour. In summer the plant bears lovely open yellow flowers about 3 inches across. Most people raise these cacti from seeds and are prepared to wait three or four years before seedlings start to move. They are exceptionally slow-growing.

Other species I have seen in collections are *C. pallida,* with globular stems, close-set short tubercles and lovely pale yellow flowers; *C. palmeri,* another globular species with close-set tubercles and pale yellow flowers; *C. elephantidens,* with rose-red flowers – it flourishes in meadows in Michoacan, Mexico; and *C. glanduligera,* which has

41

very charming yellow flowers and needs half-shade. All beautiful plants but none obtainable from any florist or nurseryman of my acquaintance. *Coryphantha* are noted for their large showy flowers. The name is from *koryphe,* summit; *anthos,* flower; referring to the position of the flowers.

*Coryphantha elephantidens*

*Echinocactus Grusonii* (named in honour of Hermann Gruson of Magdeburg, in Germany, who had a remarkable collection of cacti in that town). The generic name is derived from *echinos,* a hedgehog; and *cactus,* in reference to the spiny appearance of the plants. The popular name is the Golden Ball or the Golden Barrel Cactus; another is the Hedgehog Cactus. A delightful roundish plant covered in its young state with golden-yellow spines; later, when these turn a whitish colour, the plant is less attractive. It seldom flowers in cultivation and is prized for its 'golden ball' appearance. A native of the hot sandy regions of San Luis Potosi and Hidalgo in Mexico, where it makes a flattish-topped ball-like plant often 2 or 3 feet high and as much in diameter. Plants this size bear attractive shining yellow flowers which are about 2 inches long. They arise from new areoles at the top of the plant. This cactus in the wild is said to be used (the top sliced off) to provide sap to drink for thirsty travellers in the desert. The prominent ribs add to the attraction of these Hedgehog Cacti.

*E. ingens* (*enormous*) is much ribbed when it reaches full size, which is about 6 feet tall and as much in width. 'Bigger than a man,' is how one traveller described it. 'And you could rest against it, if it weren't

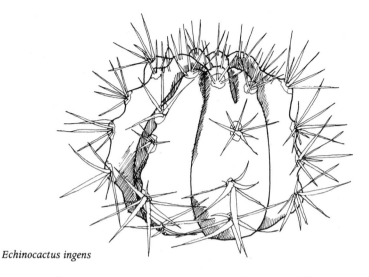

*Echinocactus ingens*

so hard and prickly – an ugly plant, like a huge growth or wart sprouting out of the earth.' But in its young state, in a pot indoors, it has very few ribs (5 or 8 – 50 or more when old) and a singularly lovely bluish frosted look (glaucous or pruinose). The areoles bear an abundance of yellowish wool; the spines are stiff and brown; the flowers small, canary-yellow within and reddish-yellow on the outside. An extremely slow-growing cactus. Lovely as a ball-shaped plant in a pot and one of those which requires full sun, winter warmth, a rich limy soil and perfectly dry conditions during the resting period. The species of *Echinocactus* are listed as 'easy to grow' cacti.

*Echinocereus* on the other hand are said to be among the rarer, more difficult kinds to grow. But this is not really the case and if you can grow the Echinocactus species successfully, you can grow any of the species of *Echinocereus* that the florists have for sale. There are three popular species. *Echinocereus Fendleri* (named in honour of August Fendler, 1813–83, who collected in New Mexico and Venezuela). The synonym is *Cereus Fendleri*. This cactus is a native of Mexico, Texas, Arizona and Utah, and makes attractive clumps of 6 inch stems, dull green and warty. The stems are ribbed and the spines very variable both in size and colour – sometimes yellow, sometimes almost black; the flowers are funnel-shaped, about 4 inches long and of a purplish violet colour. They open in the day and last for three or four days. Like the other species, *E. Fendleri* is easily increased by cuttings, by division of the clumps, or from seeds.

43

*E. Merkeri* (commemorating Gustav Merker, a Czechoslovak botanist). A native of Mexico, with erect or semi-prostrate stems which are at first green, then become grey or brown with age. They are ribbed and have prominent warts or tubercles. The spines are a glassy white colour and the flowers (as in all the species) are borne on the sides of the stems and are purplish-red and have long blunt petals. A charming cactus which looks best in a low pot or a pan.

*E. scheeri* (named in honour of Frederick Scheer, an amateur botanist who lived in England and died in 1868). Like the preceding species, it is a native of Mexico and has erect or semi-prostrate stems which are a dark glossy green. They are ribbed and have spreading white spines. The flowers are magnificent – a shade of rose-pink, big, funnel-shaped and last several days in bloom. A beautiful cactus that should be in every collection. These *Echinocereus* are said to be difficult indoor plants; but they succeed perfectly in most homes, provided they are not kept in overheated rooms. They like a cool place during the winter months. They do like a fairly rich medium (add some powdered cow manure and sifted leafmould to the soil) and they benefit from an occasional overhead watering during the growing season. People who have grown them for years find that they need more water than most other cacti and that they may be left outdoors in a place sheltered from rain till the frosts come. They are tough little plants but not hardy enough, of course, to be left outside permanently.

*Echinopsis* have been called the cacti with wonderfully fragrant flowers. The scent of some, however, is not very strong; in fact it is hardly perceptible at times; *Echinopsis chionantha*, for instance, has a very faint scent and on some days you cannot smell anything at all. A gardener who grows it tells me it should be sprayed with tepid water just before the flowers open; the scent then is stronger and reminiscent of the winter Daphne.

First, the meaning of the generic name: *Echinos*, hedgehog; *opsis*, like; the plants, round and spiny, resembling hedgehogs. *E. multiplex* (*having many parts*; probably referring to the many offsets at the base of the stem). The stem is usually a charming pale green colour, globular, and sprouts freely from the base; the ribs, about 12 in number, are straight with deep furrows between them; and from the old areoles on the sides come the flowers; these are an attractive shade of pink and very fragrant. They are large (8 inches or more in length) and have a long tube and wide, spreading, petals. An exquisite cactus, with its pink flowers and contrasting pale green stems and thick dark brown spines. A very free-flowering species (a native of southern Brazil) which does well in a small pot. (*Echinopsis* should be re-potted only when they show signs of starvation.)

*Echinopsis Eyriesii*

Two other fragrant species are *E. leucantha,* with large white flowers, which have the fragrance of violets; and the jasmine-perfumed *E. turbinata* – large white flowers streaked with green. Both are natives of Argentina.

Some of the species of *Echinopsis* are difficult to get nowadays and most nurseries, I find, stock hybrids and varieties of the plant called *E. Eyriesii,* a species with large white flowers. One of the loveliest varieties is the pink-flowered *E. grandiflora.*

Propagation of *Echinopsis* is simple – the offsets are carefully detached from the parent plants and rooted in sandy leafy soil; often you will find roots already growing from the tiny pieces.

*Epiphyllum* are cacti which grow on the trunks of trees; they are called epiphytes and derive their sustenance from decayed leaves and other debris, and by aerial roots. In cultivation we mostly grow them in hanging baskets or in ordinary pots or pans as we do the terrestrial cacti.

The word *Epiphyllum* is from *epi,* upon; and *phyllos,* a leaf, as it was thought that the flowers were borne on leaves. But the 'leaves' of course are flattish stems – see page  . Some cacti formerly known as *Epiphyllum* are now decribed under two other genera, viz. *Schlumbergera* and *Zygocactus,* the most famous being the Christmas Cactus or Crab Cactus (page 73). There are now about 16 species of *Epiphyllum* ; and a number of hybrids are offered by nurseries.

*E. Ackermannii* (named in honour of Georg Ackermann, who introduced the plant, first described as *Phyllocactus Ackermannii,* in 1834).
This cactus, which was originally said to be a native of Mexico, is now
known to be a hybrid raised in England. It is by far the most popular
*Epiphyllum* with its glorious large open dazzling crimson flowers. They
bloom by day and are much valued for indoor decoration. The main
woody stem has flat leaf-like branches, toothed or notched on each
side. There are a few spines, not very prominent, on the young growths.

*E. crenatum* (*crenate:* cut in rounded scallops; referring to the
branches). A species famous for its wonderfully-fragrant flowers,
which remain open for several days and for the fact that it is the species
largely used in raising hybrids. It is a native of Honduras and Guatemala. It has glaucous green (almost greyish) branches, flat and rather
deeply notched (crenate), and magnificent creamish-yellow flowers.

*E. phyllanthus* (*'leaf flowers'*: the flowers come on the edges of leaf-
like branches). A beautiful hanging cactus – or one that can be grown
in a hanging basket. It occurs from Panama to Paraguay, and grows
high up on tall trees; its flowers, white, 2 inches across, and with long
tubes, bloom at night; the leaf-like branches are pale green with reddish
margins. The method of growing it in a basket is quite simple: line the
basket with moss and fill it with a compost of equal parts of old leafmould, sandy loam, powdered cow manure and coarse sand.

These epiphytic cacti need a warm moist atmosphere and do best in
partial shade. They may be kept outside during hot summer weather
(the baskets suspended from branches of a tree) and should be sprayed
very frequently.

There are hundreds of different varieties or hybrids; two I came
across recently at a local florist's were TETTAUI, white flowers with
pointed petals; and USCHI, beautifully bell-shaped flowers, pale rose
in colour, with a white centre.

*Epithelantha* (one species only plus a variety called Greggii); *Erdisia*
(four species); *Eriocereus* (three species), I have been unable to obtain
from any nursery specialising in cacti, nor from any of the many florists
I have visited. *Eriocereus,* which a gardener of my acquaintance wanted
and couldn't get, is now listed under the genus *Harrisia* – many
nurseries stock *Harrisia Martinii*; and many of them *Cereus Martinii,*
which is the same.

*Erythrorhipsalis pilocarpa* is the correct name of a favourite cactus
but it is labelled in all the florists I have recently visited *Rhipsalis
pilocarpa* (this name is now the synonym).

My next, and last, 'E' cactus in the current catalogues I have at hand
is *Espostoa lanata*. Botanists describe about four species plus one or
two varieties: 'all interesting and very desirable cacti for the collector'.

46

But *E. lanata* is the only one I can get.

The genus was named in honour of Nicolas E. Esposto, a botanist who lived in Lima, Peru; *lanata* means hairy or woolly. A native of Peru and Ecuador, with erect green stems, branching at the top; the plant has many low, rounded ribs, with close areoles bearing yellowish-white glassy spines and attractive pale silky hairs which entirely cover the plant. A beautiful cactus. The flowers are white; the fruit red; neither, I think, as attractive as the silky, woolly covering. The popular name of the plant is Cotton Ball.

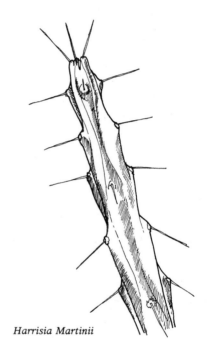

*Harrisia Martinii*

*Ferocacti,* with their long thick spines, are among the most formidable-looking of the prickly cacti – *fero* is translated as wild or very prickly. The species (about 34) are natives of Texas, California, Arizona and Mexico. *Ferocactus glaucescens* (*glaucous*) makes a large globular plant with acute ribs; it has erect yellow spines an inch or so long and funnel-shaped glossy yellow flowers which bloom for at least a week. The plant is intensely glaucous and easy to grow. These cacti need full sun in summer and an occasional watering; in winter, cool drier conditions are necessary; but they move very slowly and can remain in the same pots or pans for many years. The tiny seedlings with their overlong spines make a curious picture when massed in a pot.

*F. latispinus* (*with wide thorns or spines*) is found in eastern and central Mexico, often 9000 feet above sea-level. The radial spines (those arranged like rays) are smaller than the central ones, these being much stronger and deep red in colour. The lower one, too, is flattened and hooked at the tip. Its shape has earned the plant the name of the Devil's Tongue Cactus. The flowers are mauvish to purple and delightfully fragrant but are rarely seen on plants in cultivation.

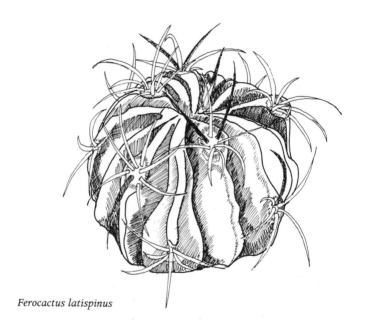

*Ferocactus latispinus*

*F. melocactiformis* is often found in collections wrongly labelled *F. meloformis* (*melon-shaped*): the correct name is given here. The specific epithet is from Latin *melo* or *melopepo,* an apple-shaped melon; and *cactus* – the stem of the plant is globular and slightly flattened at the top. This *Ferocactus* is a favourite species with collectors; it is easily raised from seed but for some years the seedlings make very slow growth. The plant body, bluish-green in colour, has a few ribs in its young state and up to 25 when it is mature. The areoles, which are spaced about an inch apart, bear clusters of spreading yellowish

48

Plate IV *Rebutia minuscula*, blooming in May. A charming cactus for a
window-sill

Plate V *Opuntia ficus-indica*, one of the hardier opuntias and sometimes grown in the open in a sheltered place

Plate VI *Lobivia pentlandii*, a cactus from Peru and Bolivia

*Gymnocalycium baldianum*

spines; and there are about 3 or 4 larger, thicker central spines. The flowers, which seldom appear on cultivated plants, are funnel-shaped, yellow within and red outside. Occasionally one comes across the plant labelled *Echinocactus Electracanthus,* which is a synonym.

*Gymnocalycium* are all natives of South America; they like a moderately-rich porous soil – usually a little extra leafmould is given them – and they like plenty of moisture in the growing season. Many of them make charming decorative plants for the home and are fairly resistant to cold weather – during a severe frost just move them to the centre of the room. The name is from the Greek *gymnos,* naked; *kalyx,* a bud, and refers to the naked flower-buds.

*G. baldianum* appears in most of the catalogues I have and is offered by many local florists; but very few botanists have described it in their works. Walter Haage does, however, in his CACTI AND SUCCULENTS; and the plants I have seen are probably the species he mentions – they were all in bloom. The plant-stems or bodies are globular, of an attractive blue-grey colour, and about $3\frac{1}{4}$ inches tall and $2\frac{3}{4}$ inches across. They have flattish ribs, which are divided into largish rounded prominences – called 'chins'. The woolly areoles bear whitish spines, dark brown at the base; and the flowers are deep purple, about 2 inches long and an inch or more in diameter; they come freely and appear in quite young plants. These flowers are self-fertile and produce plenty of seed. One of the loveliest species.

*G. gibbosum* is another, and apparently better known than *G. baldianum*. The specific epithet means 'swollen on one side'. The plant is globular but later becomes cylindrical and grows to a height of about 8 inches and measures usually $3\frac{1}{2}$ inches across. The colour is an attractive dark bluish green. The ribs are divided into chin-like tubercles; and the spines, which spread outward, are brownish – when the plant gets a lot of moisture they turn black. The flowers, about $2\frac{1}{2}$ inches long, are a charming shade of rose-pink and on well-grown plants come in profusion. There are a number of desirable varieties, most of them obtainable from nurseries specialising in cacti and succulents. My choice is var. *caespitosum* (cespitose or growing in dense clumps); the plant sprouts freely and forms groups – a valuable contrasting plant, by the way, for growing along with the single-stemmed ball-shaped cacti in an ornamental pan. Var. *nobilis,* with very prominent straight white spines which are ruby red at the base; var. *nigrum,* with a blackish-green stem and pitch black spines.

*Gymnocalycium gibbosum*

The species are natives of Argentina where the weather is often reasonably cool and moist. And, according to a specialist who grows these cacti and has collected them in their native habitats, they all benefit from being stood outside in showery summer weather for quite long periods.

*Hamatocactus setispinus* (furnished with spines) comes from Northern Mexico and Southern Texas and is one of the so-called 'easy' cacti; it grows quickly and likes a moderately rich, porous, gritty soil. There are three species and the one described here is the only one I can get from the nurseries at the moment. It is one of the loveliest of the spiny cacti. The radial spines are needle-like, white or brown and there are the thicker, longer central spines, mostly white, and hooked at the tip. The flowers, about 3 inches long and funnel-shaped, are an enchanting shining golden-yellow; they are streaked with red inside and marked on the outside with greenish-yellow. They bloom without a break from summer to late autumn – as one fades, so another opens. The stem-body, grass green in colour, is first globular, then later slightly cylindrical; the ribs are narrow and acute and notched and warty. A highly-decorative cactus, marvellously spiny, beautifully shaped and floriferous. There are several varieties; I single out the following two as the most attractive – Var. *Cachetianus:* the stem is more cylindrical, the ribs more acute, the spines are whiter and the central spine longer. Var. *hamatus,* with an oval stem; the spines are longer and the central spines brown and strongly hooked. Finally the name *Hamatocactus* (hamatus: hooked; and cactus; referring to the hooked central spine).

*Hamatocactus setispinus*

*Harrisia Martinii* (in honour of Claude Martin, 1731–1800); and the generic name commemorates William Harris, Superintendent of Public Gardens, Jamaica. The plant is often described under *Eriocereus Martinii* and this name is still used by some nurseries and florists (see page 46). Harrisias have tall-growing erect slender stems, and later they become prostrate or sprawling. Our species has areoles on its young stems, with short radial spines and a long stout central spine. The old stems are spineless. It is a night-flowering species (nocturnal) like the others, the flowers being freely produced during the summer months. They are about 8 inches long and tubular-shaped, the outer petals pale green with reddish tips, the inner petals white. A beautiful flower. The plant is a native of Argentina.

*H. Regelii,* with sweet-scented pinkish flowers, is even a lovelier plant. It flowers very freely and often gives a second show in the autumn. It is considered to be a variety of *H. Martinii* by most botanists. These cacti flourish in a fairly rich soil in places where they get plenty of sunlight all through the year. They should not be coddled in winter – the ideal temperature is about 45F (7C).

*Hylocereus undatus* (*waved or wavy*; referring to the stems, which are three-angled or wavy). The generic name is from *hyle*, wood – cereus, that inhabit woods and forests. There are 18 species, all natives of the warm wooded regions of the West Indies, Central America, Mexico and Equatorial America. They are epiphytic climbing plants with aerial roots and in cultivation need a semi-shady place in a permanently warm room and plenty of water during the summer months. *H. undatus* is the only species I am able to get at the nurseries and is known there, by the way, as *Cereus triangularis*; it is often used as stock for *Zygocactus* and other cacti. The stems are a deep green, triangular and more or less wavy; the areoles come in notches along the ribs and are wide-spaced. As in all the *Hylocereus,* the spines are small and inconspicuous. Few cacti bear such magnificent flowers; they are very large (10 inches or more in length), greenish-purple outside and the inner petals white – very beautiful. They bloom all through August and September.

A choice species I saw in bloom not long ago was *H. purpusii* (named in honour of C. A. Purpus – 1853–1941 – and his brother J. A. Purpus – 1860–1932 – German plant-collectors in Central America). The plant, an old one, grew in a pot of half sand, half leafmould, in the warm moist atmosphere of an orchid-house – the ideal place for it. The shoots, mostly three-angled, were green and very glaucous; the flowers large, with red sepals and rose-pink petals, fading with age to creamy-white. The plant climbed up trellis against a shady wall. I saw it in full bloom in late September. A really enchanting cactus when mature and flowering well. I hope the nurseries will re-introduce it.

*Lemaireocereus* (commemorating Charles Lemaire – 1801–71 – a distinguished French botanist). These cacti are usually tall, tree-like plants, with upright stems, branching from the base or with a short trunk; many bear fruits which are edible and much relished by the native people. *L. griseus* (*grey*) appears in all my catalogues as *L. eburneus,* which name is now a synonym. A tall-growing species, with prominently-ribbed stems, of a charming powdery grey colour. (The plant must not be sprayed or watered overhead or the grey-powdery colouring effect will be destroyed; water should be applied carefully to the roots.) The spines are greyish, the largest up to $1\frac{1}{2}$ inches in length. The flowers, about 3 inches long, bloom by day, and are pinkish in colour. A native of South America, and in Chile it is grown for its fruit.

*L. marginatus* (*margined*) is often grown in Central and Southern Mexico as a barrier-plant, set amongst other, usually spiny, plants to form an impenetrable screen. The stem is erect and stiff, prominently ribbed, branching from the base, dark green or grey-green in colour. The very closely-set areoles form a band or margin of contrasting grey along the crests of the ribs; the spines, at first red, are thick and inconspicuous; and the flowers, almost bell-shaped, come at the top of the stem; they are reddish within and greenish-white without. A fast-growing species (20 feet or more tall in the wild); among the most beautiful of the *Lemaireocereus*. It needs plenty of sun and always a warm, sheltered situation.

*L. stellatus* (*star-like,* referring to the radial spines) is another 'easy' cactus, and a special favourite with amateurs. The stem, columnar and branching from the base, is a dark dull green, with low ribs, which are rounded and notched. The areoles are large, with white wool; the radial spines (about $\frac{1}{2}$-inch long) spread star-like; and the central ones may be as much as $2\frac{1}{2}$ inches in length. They are all dark-coloured at first – some almost black – and then they become paler. The flowers, about $2\frac{1}{2}$ inches long, are borne at the top of the stems and a charming shade of pink. They usually last several days. The fruit is sold in the markets and much enjoyed by the natives. *L. stellatus* is grown extensively in Mexico, which is its natural home.

*Mammillaria* is a large genus consisting at present of about 150 different species – many botanists currently give the number as 'well over 200'. Some of the species formerly described under *Mammillaria* have been separated off into other genera; for instance, *M. clava* and *M. erecta,* which are both described on page 41 under *Coryphantha.* Mammillarias, commonly known as the Nipple Cacti, are well represented in nurserymen's lists and usually about two dozen different kinds are quoted.

Most species are natives of Mexico and Southern U.S.A. They are of easy cultivation, flourishing in a moderately-rich loamy soil. Some, however, prefer a sandy compost and even a gritty, stony medium. They are among the youngest cacti to bloom, and many, being shallow-rooted, prefer pans to deep pots. The flowers are small and come round the top of the stem; they bloom by day and are bell-shaped. The fruits are mostly red and very ornamental.

The generic name *Mammillaria* is from *mamilla,* a nipple, in allusion to the small tubercles.

*M. aurihamata* is a native of Central Mexico. (The specific epithet, by the way, does not appear in any of the dictionaries of plant names

I have consulted: most botanists state it has to do with the spine characters – *auri*, golden; *hamata*, hooked at the tip.) The radial spines are about ¼-inch long and yellowish-white; the central spines, four in number, are thicker, and the lower one, about 1¼ inches long, is hooked at the tip; they turn a lovely golden-yellow with age. The flowers come in a ring round the top of the stem and are a pale sulphur-yellow. The plant itself is a lovely glossy-green colour and forms stem-clusters, the stems being globular or elongated.

*M. bocasana* (from the Sierra de Bocas of Mexico) is especially common in the Bocas mountainous regions. It is the cactus often chosen by beginners because it grows so easily indoors – it is particularly amenable to pot culture – and it flowers freely. One of its great charms is its soft white covering of hair-like spines – the plant is called by some collectors the Powder Puff. The central spines stand out needle-like and are yellowish-brown in colour. The flowers, about ½-inch long, yellowish-white and striped with red, are produced at the top of the plant and over a longish period. *M. bocasana* is one of the clustering Mammillarias, the stems or stem-bodies being globular or slightly cylindric and measuring about 1½ inches across; and they are of a delightful dark bluish-green colour. You can use some of the offsets as cuttings, though some may be found to have roots; the cuttings produce a milky sap and these are left to dry for a few hours – a skin forms over the cuts – before they are inserted in pots of sandy soil.

*M. camptotricha* (*with curved or twisted hairs or spines*), a native of the Queretaro region of Mexico and an easy species to grow indoors in half-shady or sunny places. It is easily recognisable by its curved or twisted bristly spines which come in a tangle at the top of the stems. The plant forms large clumps of deep green roundish stems about 2 inches in diameter. They bear slender tubercles (nipples) about ¾-inch long; in the axils (joints) of these a few bristly hairs are produced; the curved spines are a pale yellow and an inch or so long. The flowers, fragrant, are very attractive, quite small (½-inch long); the outer petals green, the inner pure white – another favourite species with beginners.

*M. celsiana* is a native of Mexico and very common to the region of San Luis Potosi. It is one of the loveliest of the species and flourishes luxuriantly in part-shade. The stem (plant-body) roundish, is at first solitary, then later forms clumps, and is glaucous green in colour. The flowers are small (about ½-inch long) and of a bright cheerful carmine-red; they come in a ring at the top of the plant and are wonderfully decorative. I recently came across a fine specimen in bloom in a local florist's. It was 4 inches tall and about 3 inches in diameter. The tubercles were very small, the shortish spines pale yellow; the central, longer ones, sharp, prickly, a darker yellow and tipped with brown. A hint from the florist: 'Don't give the plant too much water. In the growing season give it a good soaking, then let the soil dry out, before you water again . . .

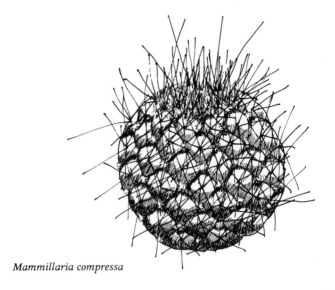

*Mammillaria compressa*

*M. compressa* (*compressed or flattened*; referring to the top of the roundish stem), a quick-growing cactus, more often than not called *M. angularis,* which name is now a synonym. The species is a native of Central Mexico and in cultivation seems to prosper well in half-shade. The plant stems, pale green and cylindric, are slightly flattened at the top; they are woolly and hairy and have a soft, ball-like appearance; the stems eventually form largish clumps. The areoles bear tiny whitish spines tipped with brown; the big central ones being about $2\frac{1}{2}$ inches long. The flowers are small, pinkish-red, and come in a ring round the top of the stems. They are freely produced in the wild but are often rare on cultivated plants.

*M. elegans* (*elegant*), a native of Central Mexico. 'The *Mammillaria* with as many synonyms as it has varieties,' says one collector. *M. dealbata* and *M. Klugii* I have seen on labels instead of the correct name *M. elegans*. There are about half-a-dozen different varieties; but Var. *supertexta* (described below) is the only one I have been able to get at present. Our species belongs to that group of Mammillarias which botanists call the *Elegantes Series:* the tubercles of these plants do not exude a milky juice when cut or damaged, the sap being found only in the internal tissues; the radial spines are very numerous; the central

55

spines sharp and prickly. The stem, about 2 inches across, is solitary, then with age begins to sprout and forms clumps. The plants are pale green, woolly and spiny at the top. The flowers come in a ring round the top and are beautifully shaded carmine red to deep violet – an enchanting little cactus for a pan and not at all difficult to grow. The variety Var. *supertexta* is an exceptionally hardy plant, with clustering sprouting stems; the flowers are a pale carmine-red and give an uninterrupted show through spring and summer.

*Mammillaria elongata*

*M. elongata* (*lengthened; elongated*) is a native of Mexico, common in the district of Hidalgo, and grows quickly in cultivation. It forms fairly large clumps of cylindrical erect stems, which are about 3 inches tall and seldom more than an inch in diameter. They are an attractive bright green and form an excellent background to the yellowish flowers (usually striped red) which come a little below the crown. The areoles bear star-like recurved yellowish spines; the central spines, one to three spread outward. There are several varieties; one of the most attractive is Var. *stella-aurata,* with slender freely-sprouting stems and golden-yellow spines, tipped with red.

*M. Hahniana* is a native of Mexico (Queretaro) and regarded as one of the finest cacti introduced in recent years. This is the *Mammillaria* species, called the white-haired counterpart of the Old Man Cactus (*Cephalocereus senilis,* described on page 38). The green globular stem, flattened at the top, is covered with white spines and with long white bristly hairs. Later the stem branches and forms clumps, giving an astonishing effect of massed white bristly hair. If we examine the tubercles closely we find that they bear up to 30 spreading soft white hair-like spines which are about $\frac{1}{2}$-inch long, and $1\frac{1}{2}$ inch central spines, which are reddish-brown at the tip. In the axils of the tubercles there are also tufts of white wool as well as about 20 longish white bristles.

*Mammillaria Hahniana*

The tubercles, by the way, unlike those of *M. elegans* (the Elegantes Series – page    ) *do* exude a milky juice when they are cut or damaged. (*M. Hahniana* belongs to the *Leucocephalae Series*.) The flowers are striking red-carmine and appear round the crown of the plant. This is a fairly hardy plant (found at 6000 feet above sea-level) and revels in full sunshine. It is easily increased by offsets or raised by seed. Most cactus nurseries can supply it.

*M. magnimamma* (literally: big breast); it is better known as *M. centricirrha*, which name, according to some botanists, means *central spine;* neither of the specific epithets, however, is very appropriate. The plant is a native of Central Mexico and is common in many regions. The plant-bodies, grey-green, are large, round, with plenty of white wool in the axils and areoles. (In time large clumps are formed and soon fill a good-sized pot or pan.) The tubercles are conical, stout, and bear recurved cream-white spines. This species is one of the free-flowering *Mammillaria,* and carries its attractive cream flowers, touched with red, round the top of the stem. It flourishes in a semi-shady place and is easily raised from seed. Collectors reckon that there are at least 100 different varieties, many of which have been given specific names. The only two I have come across are: Var. *Ehrenbergii,* which is much less branching in habit than the type; the tubercles are a deep green and covered with tiny white dots; and Var. *Krameri,* which has tubercles coloured brownish at the top and a profusion of fiery red flowers; both are probably distinct species.

*M. Mundtii* is a native of Mexico and among the freest-flowering and loveliest of all the Mammillarias. Yet the plant is not well known and for a long time I had difficulty in finding a specimen. The flowers are numerous, $\frac{3}{4}$-inch long, narrow and of a beautiful glossy carmine-red; they come in complete rings round the top of the plant. The smallest spines are white and spreading; the central ones, two in number, brown and about $\frac{3}{4}$-inch long. The plant needs full sunshine and plenty of warmth during the winter months.

*M. Petterssonii:* there are two spellings, viz. with a double *s* and with a single *s*: many botanists use the second form. And I have frequently found this cactus labelled *M. Heeseana* (the name is now a synonym). Many years ago it was something of a rarity but now it is easier to get. This species is a native of Mexico and very common in the central province of Guanajuato, the so-called Silver province – famous for its silver mines. The stem, grey-green, is globular, depressed at the centre, usually solitary (not branching), and covered at the top with long reddish spines and white wool. Later the stem becomes more cylindric. The shortest spines are white and black-tipped; the centrals chestnut brown and up to 3 inches in length. The flowers are said to be carmine-red but are rarely if ever seen.

*M. polythele (poly,* many; *thele,* nipple) comes from Mexico (Hidalgo); it is one of the cylindric-shaped Mammillarias and reaches a height of 18 inches when fully grown. The tubercles are pointed and about $\frac{1}{2}$-inch long; the axils of the young tubercles are very woolly; and the spines, about an inch long, yellowish-brown. The flowers come in a ring, the outer petals being reddish-brown; the inner petals a brilliant carmine. This cactus does best during the hot summer months in a semi-shady place; never give the plant (or any *Mammillaria*) too much water, or it will perish. All these cacti need is a frost-proof room in winter.

*M. rhodantha (with rose-coloured flowers)* grows high up on the fertile plateaus of Hidalgo (Mexico). In cultivation it prospers in a loamy open (gritty) soil containing some leafmould, and needs shading during long spells of hot sunshine. Otherwise it, and its numerous varieties, are not difficult to grow. It is a very variable species and some of the varieties are more beautiful than the type itself. Its stem, dark green, is at first cylindric, then later divides itself repeatedly into two (known as dichotomous branching – this habit is common to several other species). The tubercles are conical, their axils woolly and bristly though sometimes naked. The radial spines, about 20 in number, are white; and the central, bigger ones, reddish-brown. This cactus blooms freely, the flowers, about ½-inch across, grow in profusion in a ring near the top. They are very attractive: the outer petals are fringed and reddish-brown; the inner ones a fiery carmine-red. One of the most striking of the many varieties is Var. *Pfeifferi,* with lemon-yellow spines all slightly curved. Var. *ruberrima* is just as desirable, with exceptionally long spines of a glowing red colour.

*M. uncinata* (*uncinate, hooked*) is a native of Central Mexico (San Luis Potosi, Hidalgo) and revels in plenty of sun; it is among the hardier cacti but like all of them needs a frost-proof room through the winter months. The central spines, much stronger than the radials, are dark brown and strongly hooked; the radial spines are white, short and thick. The tubercles are milky, and the areoles bear white wool. This is a most attractive species when in full bloom, with its pinkish flowers against a background of blue-green and white. The plant-stem itself is solitary, round and depressed at the centre, up to about 3 inches high and a little more than that in width. The flowers, about ¾-inch long, come near the top and stand out beautifully against the glaucous-blue stem.

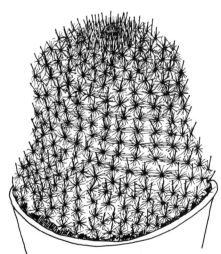

*Mammillaria vaupelii*

*M. vaupelii,* a native of Mexico, is obtainable from most cactus nurseries and is much admired for its covering of rich golden-brown spines and soft white wool – the pale green body is just visible underneath. The plant carries its small attractive purplish-pink flowers in a ring near the top. The red berries which come later in the autumn add to the charm of this species. It is one of the slow-growing Mammillarias. It needs plenty of sun and seems to prosper in quite dry soils – no watering should be done till late April.

*M. wiesingeri* is offered by most nurseries but I have not yet come across it. Most writers on cacti have omitted it from their lists. Walther Haage[1] mentions it cursorily: '*M. wiesingeri* has transparent and also reddish-brown spines, 2–2½ inch long, and rose-coloured flowers with dark stripes.' It is classed with *M. rhodantha* and is probably like that plant.

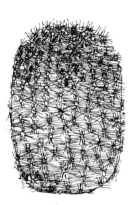

*Mammillaria wildii*

*M. wildii* is a native of Central Mexico (Hidalgo). It is easy to grow; on the whole a robust species which flowers freely throughout the summer months. It needs a good porous soil, a sunny spot and an occasional soaking during very hot summer weather. In winter it must be kept dry and in a warm atmosphere. The stems, dark or bluish-green, are cylindrical, up to 5 inches tall and about 2½ inches in diameter; they branch at the base to form clusters of erect fleshy plant-bodies. They are covered with short white bristly spines, and 3 or 4 stouter pale-yellow central spines, one of which is hooked at the tip. The flowers, ½-inch long, white with red stripes, form a crown round the top of the plant. Later the flowers are followed by bright red seed pods.

*M. woodsii* appears in one of my current catalogues as *M. woodii*: *M. woodsii* is the correct spelling. *M. woodsii* and the last species I described are both natives of Mexico (Guanajuato). *M. woodsii* is quite

[1] Author of *Cacti and Succulents,* translated by E. E. Kemp.

small, the plant-bodies, roundish, being 2 inches tall and 3 inches in diameter – in time they grow a little larger, and the stems become more cylindrical. The tubercles, $\frac{3}{4}$-inch long, are greyish-green in colour and exude a milky juice when cut, and in the axils grow white wool and long bristles. The areoles bear numerous small ($\frac{1}{4}$-inch) shining, bristly, spreading spines. And there are two erect black-tipped central spines, the larger one pointing downward. The flowers, $\frac{3}{4}$-inch long, come in a ring round the top of the plant and are an exquisite shade of carmine-red. This *Mammillaria* is easy to grow indoors and revels in full sunshine, the thick bristly covering protecting it from scorch by the hot summer sun – though no cactus should be exposed to too much heat when grown under glass or on a window-sill facing due south.

*M. Zeilmanniana* has soft, fleshy plant-stems and short hooked spines like *M. wildii* (see above), but is a bright glossy green in colour, not dark blue-green. (It belongs to the same series as *M. wildii*: a series characterised by thin radial spines, often mixed with hairs, cylindrical or narrowly conical tubercles, and central spines, straight, curved or hooked.) It is one of the most free-growing and free-flowering of all the Mammillarias. Tiny plants, $\frac{3}{4}$-inch in diameter, begin to bloom during the sunny spring weather. The tubercles are oval and closely set; the areoles, woolly when young, bear radiating white spines; the 4 central spines are reddish-brown; the lower one being slightly longer and hooked at the end. The flowers measure about $\frac{3}{4}$-inch across and are usually a deep violet-purple; they form a wonderfully decorative band round the top of the plant.

Most amateurs prefer to grow some of the Mammillarias, not only because they are comparatively easy plants – as I have already stated – but because there are always so many species and varieties to choose from in florists' and nurserymen's lists. Thirty different kinds are mentioned in one of my current catalogues – I have described some of the most interesting.

*Myrtillocactus geometrizans* comes from Central Mexico and is common in the fertile regions of Guatemala – it is used there extensively for hedging. The generic name is from *myrtillus,* a small myrtle (the diminutive of *myrtus,* the myrtle); referring to the small bilberry-like or myrtle-like fruits. The berries are gathered and sold in the country towns of Mexico; they are apparently used by the natives as raisins and are sweet and delicious.[1] The meaning of the specific epithet (*geometrizans*) according to *A Gardener's Dictionary of Plant Names* (A. W. Smith), is 'With markings arranged in a formal pattern.' This may refer to the angled ribs of the stems; these ribs are regularly spaced from each other, so regular, so precise, that they look as though a machine had carved them out. On the other hand, Professor J. Borg in

61

[1] The natives call the fruits *garambullos.*

his CACTI (London) states that the specific epithet refers to the plant's economic use, that is, 'for planting as hedges, hence the specific name.'[1] (There is however a synonym, viz. *Cereus pugionifer* (*dagger-shaped*), referring to the one central spine which is about an inch long and sword-shaped – *pugionifer* seems to be as appropriate as the other . . .)

*Myrtillocactus geometrizans*

*Myrtillocactus* is a small genus of big much-branched cacti; the main stems are stout and strong and branch out a foot or 18 inches from the ground. Our species is a favourite bedding-out cactus in the South of France, and it may be seen in large pots during the summer months standing on the terraces of some English seaside gardens. The plants, of course, are housed during the winter. The stems and branches are of a charming palish blue-green colour; the branches usually erect and 6-ribbed. The areoles (large) are spaced about an inch apart. The spines on cultivated plants are often weak and poorly developed. In nature the radial spines are spreading, less than ½-inch long; one central spine, dagger-shaped, stands out prominently and is an inch or more in length – they are all a very dark brown or black. The flowers are fragrant, small, and come in a cluster from the upper areoles; they are white and measure about an inch across. The fruit is a small round berry, blue in colour like the Whortleberry. This cactus likes a sandy leafy loam (more sand and grit than loam) and a bright sunny spot in a coolish room during hot summer days.

[1] He means the specific epithet: the specific name is the complete name – *Myrtillocactus geometrizans*.

*Notocactus;* many of these plants are now decribed under the genus *Echinocactus.* One leading horticultural dictionary says: 'NOTOCACTUS. Included in *Echinocactus*'. However, many botanists continue to describe quite a number of species and varieties, and the catalogues I have at hand list about half-a-dozen different species, and there are a dozen or more varieties. Borg says 'The genus includes 25 species, all South American.'

*N. apricus* (*sun-loving: open to the sun*) is a native of Uruguay; its habitat is sandy grassy land exposed to the hot sun and swept by winds from the Atlantic. A charming species, with a round stem, $2\frac{1}{2}$-inches across, which forms groups of plants round its base. It is pale green and covered with reddish-yellow spines which extend completely over the crown of the plant. The plant body has numerous ribs which are slightly notched. The radial spines are bristle-like and curved; and the central spines are stouter and about $1\frac{1}{4}$ inches long. This species is magnificent in flower. The flowers themselves are large, about 3 inches long, with a thick tube covered with white wool and bristles; the petals are yellow marked with red. *Notocactus* flourish luxuriantly in porous, slightly acid soils (use 2 parts of powdered peat or leafmould to 1 part of sandy, coarse gritty loam). The plants need plenty of water in the growing season but should be kept on the dry side all through the winter. Half shade is better than full sun when the plants are in bloom. The flowers usually last several days.

*N. concinnus* (*neat; elegant; well-made*) – you may take your choice: the plant is all these. It is a beauty and a special favourite with cactus-lovers. The flowers are magnificent: funnel-shaped, about $2\frac{1}{2}$ inches long, a shining lemon-yellow with red stripes; the petals outside are carmine with dark red markings. Quite young plants bloom. The flowers come at the top of the plant and stand up beautifully above the glossy green round stems, which are about $2\frac{1}{2}$ inches tall and 4 inches in diameter. These are ribbed, the ribs notched into warts. The radial spines are pale yellow and bristle-like; there are 4 central spines, yellowish or reddish, the lower one, thick at the base and about $\frac{3}{4}$-inch long. *N. concinnus* revels in full sunshine; it comes from the hot sunny regions of Southern Brazil and Uruguay.

*N. Haselbergii,* another species from Southern Brazil. Many botanists describe the plant under the genus *Malacocarpus.* It is among the smaller cacti; the stem is sometimes slightly cylindrical, up to 5 inches tall, with a diameter of 4 inches or so when the plant is fully grown. It is flat at the top and this area is completely covered with soft white spines, which are tipped with yellow. The ribs are divided into low roundish tubercles about $\frac{1}{4}$-inch apart. The areoles are small, with white wool, the top ones producing the flowers. The radial spines are needle-like,

63

yellowish-white and very short; the centrals, usually 4 in number, up to $\frac{3}{4}$-inch long and golden-yellow at first, then a paler shade. Many of the Notocacti give a good show of flowers, these lasting several days; our species is in bloom for a week or more; its flowers, about $\frac{3}{4}$-inch long and $\frac{1}{2}$-inch across, are a striking fiery orange-red: and I have known them to last 10 or 12 days. Propagation is by seed; the seedlings (very slow in growth) are then grafted on *Trichocereus Spachianus,* a tall beautiful, night-blooming cactus from Western Argentina (see page 73). Occasionally this species sprouts from the base, producing small offsets. It is easy to grow and does best during hot summer days on a shady window-sill.

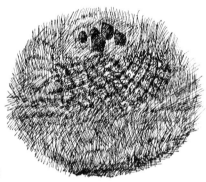

*Notocactus Haselbergii*

diameter; it is often tortuous (having an irregular, meandering mode of growth). The flowers come at the top (like a cap) and are two inches across – they are a glossy yellow within and streaked with green on the outside – unfortunately they don't appear till the plant reaches a certain height; but the stem-shape is always interesting and pleasing to see. The stem is ribbed, the ribs slightly notched, and the areoles when young bear whitish wool. The top is also covered with whitish wool and long hair-like golden spines. The radial spines, about $\frac{1}{4}$-inch long, are pale yellow; and the central ones (three or four) are $1\frac{1}{2}$ inches long, bristle-like, golden-yellow and arched backward. Specialist nurseries tell me that this *Notocactus* is the most popular species and that there is always a great demand for it. It is comparatively easy to grow indoors. It prefers a partially-shady place and should be kept on the dry side all through the year. All Notocacti much appreciate a longish spell outdoors in midsummer. *N. Leninghausii,* like the species above, comes from the hot dry regions of Southern Brazil.

*Notocactus Leninghausii*

*N. Leninghausii* – in shape this species is the opposite of *N. concinnus*: it is tall, cylindrical, up to 3 feet in height and about 4 inches in

*N. Ottonis* (in honour of Eduard Otto – 1812–1885 – collector in Cuba and Venezuela; or his father Friedrich Otto – 1782–1856 – curator of the Berlin Botanic Garden). This species is found in Southern Brazil, Uruguay, Paraguay and Argentina and its wide distribution has given us a number of different varieties all very attractive; one or two are mentioned below. *N. Ottonis* has a lovely glossy green stem (plant-body), about $4\frac{1}{2}$ inches across when fully grown, and is spiny and woolly at the top. Occasionally the plant sprouts from the base. The ribs, about 13 in number, are straight and more or less notched. The areoles bear slender, yellow radial spines and stout central spines of a reddish-brown colour. The flowers, funnel-shaped, up to $2\frac{1}{2}$ inches long, are a deep golden-yellow and last in bloom for several days. This species flowers very freely and has been in cultivation since the early nineteenth century. Of the many beautiful varieties I choose Var. *multi-florus,* which has masses of flowers during the summer; Var. *paraguay-ensis,* with conspicuous red spines; and Var. *uruguayensis,* a robust plant with broad round ribs.

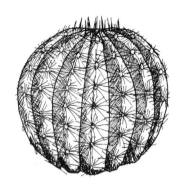

*Notocactus Ottonis*

*N. rutilans* (*reddish;* probably referring to the reddish-brown spines): this species according to Walther Haage was first introduced to Switzerland in 1936 and was not described till 1948. It is missing from many standard works on cacti; but most nurseries have the plant – some spell the name *N. rutlens.* This cactus has a small globular or sometimes slightly elongated stem of an attractive blue-green colour. The plant is deeply ribbed, and the ribs are divided into smallish tubercles. At first the areoles bear white wool but later become naked. The radial spines are very short, less than $\frac{1}{4}$-inch long, usually white, though sometimes tipped with red. There are two central spines, about $\frac{1}{2}$-inch long and of a light reddish-brown colour. Many nurseries advertise this species as having the most beautiful flowers of all the Notocacti; they are very striking – 2 inches across, deep carmine on the outside, and a bright golden-yellow within. A lovely plant. This species comes from the extreme west of Uruguay, close to the Brazilian border.

*N. scopa:* two varieties are offered, viz. Var. *candida,* with white spines tipped pink when young – a popular plant with cactus collectors; and Var. *ruberrima,* which has shining ruby-red central spines – more attractive than the other, I think. The type (the species itself) is round in shape at first, then becomes more cylindric, up to about 5 inches tall and $2\frac{1}{2}$ inches thick; the plant occasionally sprouts from the base. The ribs are low and notched into smallish warts or tubercles. The plant has been called one of the white, woolly, spiny cactuses (I recall an enthusiastic collector's remarks) – but is not particularly floriferous: older plants bloom more freely. The areoles, spaced $\frac{1}{4}$-inch apart, are white and woolly when young; and they bear up to 40 very slender $\frac{1}{4}$-inch snow-white radial spines. The 3 or 4 central ones are stouter, longer and usually dark brown in colour. The flowers, 2 inches long, come from the centre of the stem and are a bright lemon-yellow with a contrasting vivid red stigma (the organ that receives the pollen in impregnation). Both the species and the varieties I have mentioned prosper in a fairly rich (leafy, loamy) soil, in a sunny spot during the growing season; but need protection from prolonged spells of scorching heat (stand the plant outside on exceptionally hot days). Keep the soil moist during spring and summer and on the dry side all through the late autumn and winter. Like the other Notocacti, this species is a native of tropical South America – Southern Brazil and Uruguay.

*Opuntia* comes next in the catalogues, but this genus does not belong to the CEREEAE TRIBE or Group but to the OPUNTIEAE TRIBE (see page 32); and about 15 species are listed; these and the one other TRIBE, viz. the PERESKIEAE TRIBE which has only one genus) are described in the next chapter. We continue here with the half-dozen or so remaining genera of the CEREEAE Group. And our next plant is *Oreocereus Celsianus* (*oreo-*, a mountain; and Cereus); the popular name is Mountain Cereus; the various species – about 5 in number – are found on the eastern slopes of the Andes, from Peru and Bolivia to Chile. This is a highly-ornamental plant for a tropical or a semi-tropical garden, and may be seen growing in special beds in the south of France and in gardens along the coast of the Italian Riviera. The botanist Haage mentions a new name, viz. *Oreocereus neocelsianus;* but nurseries and florists mostly retain the old one. The plant has an erect stem, up to about 3 feet tall and 5 inches thick; the stem branches at the base or a few inches above ground level. The colour is dark green; the ribs are notched into tubercles and clothed with long white wool and clusters of small yellowish spines and longer, thicker central spines; the long silky white hairs which come from the upper areoles often hide most of the spines and remind one of the Old Man Cactus (see page 38) – there is, in fact, a species of *Oreocereus*, with an abundance of long, whitish hairs; its popular name is Old Man of the Andes.[1] The flowers of our species are produced near the top of the stem, often 3 or 4 inches long and of an uncommonly beautiful shade of reddish-brown. Like all the long-haired cacti, the hairy *Oreocereus* need protection from the dirt and grime that float in the air; it is a simple matter, however, to wash the hairs (see page 38). There are two very attractive varieties; Var. *Bruennowii*, with more slender stems than the type, and covered with matted, brownish woolly hairs – described by a collector as the 'untidiest-looking of all the long-haired cacti . . .'; and Var. *Williamsii*, with densely-woolly stems; the spines are white or pale yellow and up to $\frac{3}{4}$-inches long.

*Oreocereus* need a soil containing plenty of lime, best supplied by crushed limestone or – recommended by some specialists – crushed

[1] This is the species *O. Trollii* from the Andes of Bolivia; the hairs, up to $2\frac{1}{4}$ inches long, creamy-white and silky, completely cover the stem. The flowers

marble chippings. Add it to a compost of 2 parts each of leafy garden loam and sand. The plants do well on a warm, sunny window-sill; they need watering regularly during the growing season and a fairly dry soil and a cool atmosphere in winter.

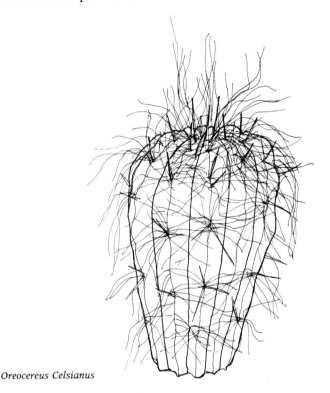

*Oreocereus Celsianus*

*Pilocereus chrysomallus*: the genus has now been discarded but the name still appears in many catalogues; the plant is now described under *Pachycereus chrysomallus* by the vast majority of writers. *Pachycereus* is a genus of giant tree-like cacti which often surpass in size the huge *Carnegiea gigantea* of Arizona (page 36). There are 10 different species, natives of Mexico and Lower California, some forming vast forests that provide shade and shelter for travellers: strange, ribbed trees, one man described them, that looked as if they had been turned to stone. There is an architectural quality about them which the foreigner finds singularly fascinating – weird, artificial-looking giants, the like of which can be seen nowhere else in the world. *Pachycereus chrysomallus* (*pachys*, thick; referring to the stout stems); and the specific epithet: according to the botanist Borg (CACTI, page 159); 'The flowering stems develop at the top masses of long wool of a yellowish brown colour, like a helmet, hence the specific name . . .' (epithet?) – *chrysos* – gold or golden. . . . In nature this huge cactus reaches a height of between 30 and 40 feet, with a stem 5 or 6 inches thick, and forming a dense crown of erect branches light green in colour. They are ribbed, with closely-set tubercles; the areoles are furnished with yellowish wool and small brown radial spines; the central spines are about an inch long. The caps or tops of massed golden wool are very attractive – the small bell-shaped cream flowers much less so. These, by the way, appear only on old plants.

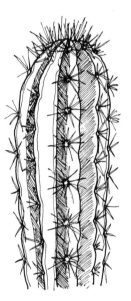

*Pachycereus Pringlei*

*P. Pringlei* (named in honour of C. G. Pringle of Vermont, U.S.A., who collected in Mexico, *c*. 1887). One of the biggest of the *Pachycereus*, a giant cactus whose stem or trunk often measures 3 feet in diameter at the base. The stem of this magnificent plant begins branching at 3 feet or so from the ground and is an attractive dark green. The stems are ribbed, the ribs closely studded with large areoles, which are furnished with short grey wool and numerous spines, mostly white with black tips. The flowers are roughly funnel-shaped and greenish-white; the fruits are round and covered with wool and yellowish spiny bristles. *Pachycereus* need a sandy gritty soil and plenty of sun during the growing season. Our cultivated plants can only ever be

69

miniatures: we must travel a very long way if we want to see these giant cacti in their full splendour, nurtured by the sun and rain of the deserts. Collectors who have a special cactus-house can grow fairly large specimens; good-sized seedlings can often be obtained from the nurseries. Cuttings do not strike readily and seeds take too long to grow and mature.

*Rebutia*. In size and height these cacti are the extreme opposite of the *Pachycereus* – they are exiguous plants, some not an inch tall and ideally suited to pot culture; indeed, you can grow several different kinds in a single pan. They make excellent companion plants, too, for some of the Mammillarias (page 53). The genus is named in honour of P. Rebut, a French cactus dealer. With the constant introduction of new species (natives of South America) the genus now consists of between 30 and 40 different species – originally there were about half a dozen.

*Rebutia Marsoneri*

*Rebutia Marsoneri* is one of the newer species, a small round plant, which branches round the base and has exquisite golden-yellow open flowers. The plant much resembles a *Mammillaria* and has spirally-arranged tubercles or warts with yellowish spines. This species is a native of Argentina: first discovered in the Province of Jujuy bordering on Chile. It is not so well known, nor so popular, as the following two species.

*Rebutia minuscula* (very small) comes from Tucuman, Northern Argentina. 'Like a jewel or some precious ornament by Fabergé' says one collector. It is a lovely plant and worth a place in anybody's collection of exotics for indoor decoration. The plant-body or stem is about an inch high and two inches in diameter; it is glossy green, with tubercles arranged spirally in 20 rows; the areoles bear tiny white or pale yellow spines with a prominent central spine, which is less than ¼-inch long. The flowers sprout from round the base of the stem and bloom through spring and summer. They are funnel-shaped, 1½ inches long, ¾-inch wide and a brilliant red; they open in the morning and close toward evening, lasting three or four days. They appear on and off for several months, even on one-year-old plants. It is an easy cactus to grow, prospering in part-shade and needing a cool sunny place in winter. The variety *multiflora* is a favourite plant; it blooms freely several times in April and May and then again in late summer.

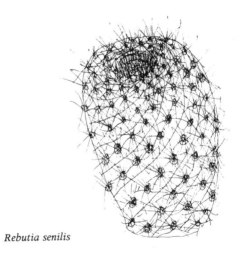

*Rebutia senilis*

*R. senilis* (*aged, hence white-haired*; referring to the hair-like glassy-white spines); from the Province of Salta in Northern Argentina. This is a larger plant, with a roundish stem (depressed at the top) about 3 inches high and the same in diameter. The stem is a pale green; the bristles which cover the plant are about an inch long, shining white and show up the funnel-shaped, carmine-red flowers to perfection. There are a number of beautiful varieties: Var. *aurescens*, with yellow bristles covering the top. Var. *cana*, with dull white spines. Var. *lilacino-rosea*, a charming plant with lilac-pink flowers. And a special

71

favourite: Var. *Stuemeriana*, which has larger flowers than the type – they are yellowish-red with a yellowish throat.

You can increase your stock of Rebutias simply by planting seed, which you can gather from your own plants: they produce plenty. The fruits are small berries; these split open and reveal the minute black seeds. Often tiny seedlings will be found springing up round the parent plant, the seeds having fallen there and germinated. Germination occurs within a few days. Another method is to divide the rootstock, which sprouts and forms offsets. This job must be done in summer and care taken that neither the main plant nor the offsets are damaged or torn in separating them. The offsets or cuttings are then rooted in a shady place in a mixture of sand and powdered leafmould.

*Trichocereus pasacana* (*trichos,* hair; plus *cereus* – the flowering parts are hairy). In nature this is a magnificent columnar cactus, with stems up to 15 feet tall and 2 feet or more thick. The plant is bright green, with broad, low, rounded ribs (20 to 35), and brown areoles furnished with 4inch stiff, brownish spines. The areoles at the top of the stems bear long white bristles; and those on the sides produce the flowers, these being about 4 inches long, funnel-shaped, white, very showy and opening at night. The fruits, which are edible, are round and green and called *pasacana* by the natives. *T. pasacana* comes from North-western Argentina and Bolivia. It is a robust but slow grower in cultivation. It revels in a sunny place and is mostly raised from seed.

*Trichocereus Spachianus*

*T. Spachianus* (in honour of the Alsatian botanist, Edouard Spach – 1801–1879). This species blooms only when it has reached maturity, then the flowers come very freely and round the top of the stems; they are greenish-white in colour, about 8 inches long and open at night and often remain in bloom till late morning. The stem of this cactus when fully grown is usually over 5 feet tall and about 2½ inches thick; it branches freely from the base. It is an attractive light green colour and has 10 to 15 rounded ribs, with areoles set close together, bearing yellowish, bristle-like spines about ½-inch long; the centrals, usually one or two are slightly longer. This species is frequently used as stock for grafting. Unlike the previous species and *T. strigosus*, it flourishes more luxuriantly in soil containing very little lime: most *Trichocereus* prefer a large admixture of lime-rubble.

*T. strigosus* (*with stiff bristles*) is noted for its coloured spines and also for its large flowers, which are often fragrant and exhale a scent reminiscent of rich, fruity magnolia. (Many of the *Trichocereus* have scented flowers; some are listed as having slightly fragrant flowers, but often it is impossible to perceive any scent from them). This species, a native of North-western Argentina, prospers very well in cultivation but unfortunately doesn't flower readily. The flowers, white and of an exquisite satiny appearance, last in bloom for a day or so, and open from buds growing from tufts of deep golden hairs on the sides of the mature stems. The plant itself has an erect stem 3 feet or more in height and 3 inches thick, grey-green in colour, and ribbed; the ribs, 15 to 18, are low and rounded. The spines, which are numerous, are very variable in size and colour: ranging from greyish-white through yellow and yellowish-red to dark red; the largest (the centrals) are up to 2 inches long. There are several varieties – Var. *intricatus*, with long crimson spines; Var. *longispinus* has longer spines, blood-red in colour when young; Var. *variegatus*, with yellow or red spines which are tipped brown. *T. strigosus* and its varieties, along with *T. pasacana* (page 72) like full sun and a limy soil, but not, as some amateur growers believe, a thin, starved soil (desert soil); it must be in good heart and have lime-rubble added. All *Trichocereus* benefit from being sprayed frequently with tepid rain water during the growing season.

Our last cactus of the CEREEAE GROUP is the famous Crab or Christmas Cactus – *Zygocactus truncatus* (see pages 12 and 34). The generic name is from the Greek *zygon*, a yoke, plus *Cactus*, probably referring to the jointed stems. The specific epithet, *truncatus*, means cut off square – the ends of the shoots have the appearance of being sliced across. You may find that this cactus is labelled by some florists as *Epiphyllum truncatum*, which was the original specific name (see page 45). In the wild the Crab Cactus grows on the trunks of trees and on shady stony shelves in the Organ Mountains in the state of Rio de Janeiro (Eastern Brazil), as do several other genera of epiphytic cacti – *Epiphyllum*, *Schlumbergera*, etc. The stems of the Crab Cactus are flattened and jointed and branch dichotomously (divide into two). These flat, leaf-like joints – crab-claw joints – are from $1\frac{1}{2}$ to 2 inches long; the margins are serrate (notched) and the areoles at the end bear wool, bristles and the flowers. The latter, up to 3 inches long, are variable in colour, several natural forms being listed: pink, red, deep claret and an almost pure white. The tube curves upward, the stamens and pistil stand out conspicuously and the petals (perianth leaves) are reflexed.

This cactus is greatly valued by growers of exotics for indoor decoration on account of its late blooming period; it is usually at its best from October to January – often in full bloom at Christmas.

But although many people grow it, few seem to know how to look after it really well. First and foremost, it needs more fresh air treatment than it usually gets; indeed, it should be stood outside in a shady, sheltered spot whenever there is no sign of frost. So, often – especially in warm maritime districts – it can be left in the open from late April till the beginning of October. Then, when the buds begin to form, the plant must be brought indoors to help on the development of the flowers; this cactus needs a reasonably high temperature during the flowering season. During the summer months the plants should be syringed every other day with tepid rain water; leave the water in the sun for several hours before you use it. It is a shade-loving plant and shade is easy enough to provide indoors during the winter. It also needs a warm moist atmosphere; again, the right temperature is easy to provide; and the moisture should be supplied by spraying with tepid water: stand the plant in the sink and spray it there to avoid making a mess in the room. Grow this *Zygocactus* (the only species, by the way) in a compost made up of equal parts of sifted leafmould or peat, old powdered cow manure, sandy garden loam crushed bricks, and crushed charcoal.

Propagation is often affected by cuttings: early in the year insert pieces 2 inches long consisting of two or three segments of stem in sandy leafmould in a shady place; they will root by the autumn. The favourite method, however, is to graft young pieces of shoots on *Pereskia aculeata* (a cactus described in the next chapter);[1] these grafted plants are grown to standards and the long main stems show off the hanging flowers to best advantage. In full bloom *Zygocactus truncatus* is the most arresting of all the easier cacti to grow.

74

[1] Another cactus used for grafting is *Hylocereus undatus* (see page 52).

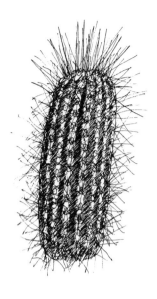

*Trichocereus strigosus*

*Zygocactus truncatus*

# Chapter Three
# Opuntias
# and *Pereskia Aculeata*

*Opuntias* are the best known of all cacti and the most curiously shaped. And – something perhaps not every gardener knows – *Opuntia* is the largest genus (of about 135 cacti genera): it comprises over 300 different species. Most catalogues list about 20. There are plenty to choose from, then, and some in their young state are small enough to grow in a pan along with other cacti, preferably of contrasting shapes.

Opuntias are natives of America, from the states of Utah and Nebraska, in the centre of U.S.A. down to Patagonia, at the extreme South of South America, where, a recent traveller to the region tells me, there are extensive plains covered with coarse grasses and sparse scrub, and many desert regions utterly desolate, except for the bizarre vegetation of the Opuntias. He, an amateur collector, was able to identify three or four of the species he saw. (None is listed in any catalogue).

First, *Opuntia Darwinii*, a crawling or procumbent cactus with smooth, grey-green ovalish joints about $1\frac{1}{2}$ inches in length. The spines occur only at the top (one to three) and are as long as the joints, yellow in colour and they come from large areoles which are also furnished with wool and glochids, both yellowish. The fruits had large woolly areoles; he did not describe the flowers – these happen to be a deep yellow. In removing some of the fruits, a few glochids (minute bristle-like spines intermixed with the spines – see page 10) penetrated the top of his forefinger; they were painful but easily scraped off with a sharp pen-knife. (They are not poisonous, as is sometimes supposed).

The second he mentioned was *O. platyacantha* (*broad-spined*); this opuntia is also found in Chile. It is rare in collections, I believe; it belongs, with the other – *O. Darwinii* – to the *Opuntia* Section known as TEPHROCACTUS (dull green or ashy green cactus); these are the most interesting kinds but the most difficult in cultivation. This was another low, prostrate cactus with ovalish joints (dull green or brownish-green); the areoles were large, yellow; spines $1\frac{1}{2}$ inches long, some of them flat and leathery. The flowers were yellow. There are apparently several varieties in cultivation.

The third was *Opuntia Salmiana*, which is also found in South Brazil and Northern Argentina. This is a different kind: a taller-growing plant, usually about $1\frac{1}{2}$ feet high but sometimes twice as tall. It has long, smooth, cylindrical stems, which branch freely, and are of a deep glaucous-green. The areoles are tiny, with numerous glochids and yellowish spines. The flowers, also numerous, are yellow and with age turn reddish-orange. The fruits are red and about $\frac{1}{2}$-inch in diameter. There were also various species of *Pterocactus*, low cacti, branching from the ground (included in the OPUNTIEAE GROUP or TRIBE).

The Opuntias offered by florists and nurserymen are the easier ones to grow and do well in pots indoors; and the hardiest ones are suitable for outdoor cultivation in some warm sheltered places. In some European countries – France and Italy, for instance – they are grown permanently in the open and are a feature of many of the pleasure gardens along the shores of the Mediterranean.

*Opuntia Bergeriana*

*Opuntia Bergeriana* (probably named in honour of Alwin Berger, 1871–1931, Curator of the garden at La Mortola and writer on succulents). This Opuntia is not known in the wild, Borg says: 'Described from specimens at the Riviera: native country unknown. . . .' In the south of France it is in full bloom in May as a rule. It flowers freely, the flowers being deep red, the stamens dark pink, the stigma white and the lobes green. The fruits are about 2 inches long, pear-shaped, red in colour, but not edible. This species when fully grown is tree-like and has spreading branches, with ovalish grey-green joints, 7 to 10 inches long. The areoles are about an inch apart and bear yellow glochids and brown or yellow spines of varying length, the longest measuring $1\frac{1}{2}$ inches. *O. Bergeriana* is a strong grower and forms rather untidy-looking thickets wherever it has been planted in the warmest countries of Southern Europe. Small plants can be obtained in pots from most florists and cactus-nurseries.

Several of the more robust Opuntias have become naturalised in many hot countries of the world. Some kinds, such as *O. microdasys*, are often damaged, however, by a prolonged spell of cold; and snow and frost are, of course, known in the Mediterranean territories. But this particular Opuntia – and many others – are not pestiferous plants as are the creeping vigorous kinds that are a fearful and colonizing menace in some parts of Australia. (It is well known that scientists controlled this spreading ruin by introducing the cactoblast, a South American moth whose larvae killed off the plants.) *O. vulgaris*, now more frequently called *O. opuntia*, is found growing wild by the sides of the roads between Rome and Naples and in other parts of Italy and in Switzerland – its habitat extends from Massachusetts to Virginia and to Ontario in Canada. It has been given the popular name of Indian Fig, though this really belongs to *O. Ficusindica*, a native of tropical America. Botanists in the nineteenth century confounded one with the other. William Rhind, writing about 1860, mentions the introduction of the India Fig into England and states it was fruited in the open (by Braddoch near London) about that time – the specific name he gives to this cactus is *Cactus Opuntia*, a synonym of *Opuntia opuntia*. Neither *O. opuntia* nor *O. Ficus-indica* is commonly grown in pots for indoor decoration; but *O. monocantha*, sometimes called *O. vulgaris*, is offered by most nurseries.

*O. crassa* is a much more suitable species for collectors and described by nurseries as a beautiful cactus much resembling *O. microdasys*, but it is hardier than that plant. *O. crassa* (*thick*) is a native of Mexico and makes a straggling bush about $3\frac{1}{2}$ feet tall. Its oval, almost rounded, joints are up to $4\frac{1}{2}$ inches long, about 3 inches broad and $\frac{1}{2}$-inch thick. They are grey-green (or glaucous), fleshy-looking (*crassa* also means fleshy); smooth or sometimes slightly downy and thickly studded with large brownish areoles bearing tufts of shining brownish-yellow glochids. The spines, usually one or two, are tiny and often absent from cultivated plants. The flowers are yellow; the fruits large and edible.

O. *Engelmannii* (in honour of Georg Engelmann – 1809–1884 – German-born St. Louis physician and a brilliant botanist).[1] This is a big bush-like plant, with round, thick, pale green joints up to 12 inches long. The areoles are very prominent (bulging outward) creamy-white in colour, and bear yellow glochids and white spreading spines which are brown or red at the base; the longest measure about 2 inches and are flattened. The flowers are yellow and 3 to 4 inches across. The fruits are variable: sometimes round or oval, sometimes pear-shaped (the popular name Prickly Pear is perhaps better known than Indian Fig;) they are usually about $1\frac{1}{2}$ inches long. There are one or two varieties – the only one I have seen so far is Var. *dulcis*, a prostrate form with small joints and delicious sweet-flavoured fruits. The species is found in Mexico, New Mexico, Arizona and Texas.

O. *microdasys* (*small-shaggy*) was mentioned on page 78. It is not listed in any catalogue I have at hand, but two of its varieties are – Borg describes the type as 'very lovely and popular. . . .' Var. *albispina* (*with white spines*: actually glochids in this plant); it has rounded or ovalish joints about 3 inches long and rather thin. The areoles and tufts of glochids are an enchanting shining silvery white. The popular name mentioned in one of the catalogues is Angel's Wings. It is a beautiful plant, smaller than the type. A native of Mexico and seems to suffer if left in unheated rooms during the winter months.

Var. *rufida* (*pale red, becoming brown*) is given specific rank by some botanists. It is a native of Northern Mexico and Texas. A popular name is Red Bunny Ears – I suppose the joints resemble ears. The joints are ovalish, about 3 inches long, with large areoles bearing red or chocolate-brown glochids; there are no spines. This is a charming cactus, erect and about 18 inches tall, for growing in a pot and at its loveliest when its orange-yellow flowers are in full bloom. (*Opuntia* flowers are cup- or saucer-shaped and mostly yellow-orange or red-orange).

O. *monacantha* (*one-spined*) is a native of Southern Brazil, Uruguay, Paraguay and Argentina and according to some writers 'A tall form of O. *vulgaris* . . .' (see page 78). In nature this cactus reaches a height of between 6 and 7 feet. The joints, which are oval or sometimes more elongated, narrow considerably at the point where they come from the mother joint; they vary from 4 inches to 12 inches in length and are an attractive glossy green in colour. The areoles, widely spaced,

[1] 'He was first to call attention to the immunity of American grape stocks to phylloxera. This virtually saved the European wine industry.' *A Gardener's Dictionary of Plant Names*. A. W. Smith.

are furnished with one straight spine 1½ inches long; on the top joints there are sometimes two or three; the flowers, deep yellow, with the outer petals red at the base, measure 3 inches across and contrast well with the glossy green joints. The fruits, up to 3 inches long are red, pear-shaped and proliferous, that is, they later develop new fruits from the aeroles on the fruits.

There are two varieties, viz. Var. *variegata*, with smaller joints exquisitely marbled white or yellow and often pink – a very desirable Opuntia for a pot indoors. And Var, *Lemaireana*, which also has smaller joints and smaller flowers but many more of these than the type plant.

*O. prolifera* (*proliferous*) is a native of Southern California and Lower California. The fruits, which are seedless, are freely proliferous. The flowers are small, about 2 inches long and 1½ inches across, bright red and very showy. This is a bushy plant, varying in height (in the wild) from 3 feet to about 6 foot 6 inches and is much-branched, quickly making impenetrable thickets. The joints are a rich green, varying in length from 1½ inches to 5 inches, and they are about 1½ inches thick and fleshy-looking. A succulent plant that makes you want to prick it to watch the juice run. The glochids are yellow-brown; and the spines (6 to 12) are about ½-inch long. A charming cactus for a small pot.

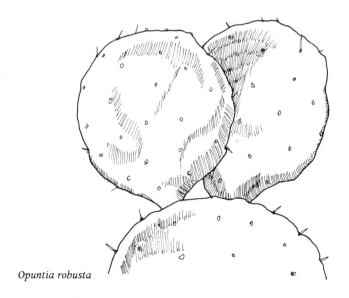

*Opuntia robusta*

Plate VII *Agave americana variegata*,
a fine foliage plant for a warm
garden in the south

Plate VIII *Mesembryanthemum edule*, a charming succulent from sunny South Africa

Plate IX *Euphorbia splendens*, the Crown of Thorns plant, a spiny, succulent shrub with showy, scarlet flowers

*O. robusta* (*stout; strong in growth*) in its habitat (Central Mexico) grows to tree-size and produces enormous, almost round, joints 8 to 10 inches long, the biggest being 12 inches broad – sometimes 15 inches on plants growing in the South of France. The joints are grey-green and quite smooth, with a most attractive bluish-white bloom. (A form called Var. *camuessa* is grown in Mexico specifically for its fruit). In cultivation, *O. robusta* is a very different plant: it is often spineless and lacks its glaucous colouring and, of course, it is much smaller. (It is listed in most catalogues and recommended for indoor decoration.) The spines on natural plants are thick, yellow and 2 inches long; the flowers, yellow and 2½ inches broad; the fruits, dark red, round and about 3 inches long. A magnificent cactus for a tropical garden. It is often associated with *O. Ficus-indica* and grown in conjunction with that species. *O. Ficus-indica* (*Ficus* means Fig) is the Indian Fig, grown for its delicious fruits. It is also tree-like (up to 15 feet tall), a native of Tropical America and grown and naturalised in many warm countries of the world. In fully mature plants the joints – often spoon-shaped – are sometimes 20 inches long, green, not glaucous; the flowers canary-yellow; and the fruits oval or pear-shaped, up to 4 inches long. Of the half dozen varieties listed by botanists Var. *lutea*, with oval yellow fruits, is the sweetest and most delicious.

*O. subulata* (awl-shaped); this is one of the cacti that produces leaves (see page 10); these are awl-shaped,[1] up to 5 inches long and come from large, grooved tubercles or warts. In the grooves are aeroles bearing one or two pale yellow, short, strong spines, intermixed with a few yellow glochids. The plant makes a tall shrub (up to 12 feet or so) in the wild, well branched, with cylindrical, dark green stems or joints, and attractive large red flowers. The fruits are ovalish in shape, green and often proliferous. The species, a native of Chile and Argentina, has produced a charming variety – Var. *minor*, a cactus smaller in all its parts. Both are excellent for growing in pots indoors.

*O. sulphurea* (*sulphur-yellow*; referring to the colour of the flowers), a native of Argentina (common in the district of Santiago) and a popular cactus with growers. I have seen three different specimens in full bloom, belonging to cactus enthusiasts. None was more than 10 inches tall, which is about half the height of the wild plant – and they were all apparently about 10 years old. This species is decidedly a desert plant; that is, it likes really dry conditions and, from information given me, suffers if given too much water. In the desert rocky country where it grows it makes a straggling bush about 18 inches tall and is often much wider than that. The joints, 3 to 7 inches long, are flat and fleshy, usually oval-shaped, and green with a reddish tinge; they are tuberculate, the tubercles being broad and bearing areoles furnished

[1] Awl-shaped: Narrow and attenuate (becoming thinner) from a broader base to a slender or rigid point.

with yellowish-red glochids and 2 to 8 spines, brownish red, the long-est measuring 4 inches. The flowers are large and a charming shade of sulphur yellow. This Opuntia is a special favourite with collectors.

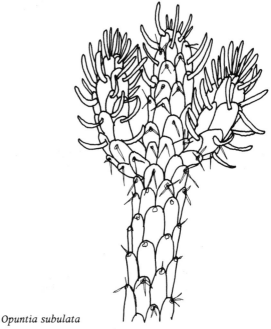

*Opuntia subulata*

*O. tomentosa (densely woolly; with matted hair)* is a native of Central Mexico and an escape (a garden plant growing wild) in parts of Australia. This species, tree-like in the wild, has dark green, narrowly-oval joints 4 or 5 inches in length, often longer, and densely covered with velvety down. The areoles are widely spaced and have a few pale yellow glochids; often the spines are absent; occasionally there are one or two, these being very short and white. The flowers are an arresting shade of red, glowing, and show up beautifully above the dark velvety green stems. They are quite small, 2 inches across; the fruits are oval, dark red and spineless. This species is often used as a rootstock for grafting those Opuntias that are slow or make only weak growth in cultivation.

*O. tuna* (West Indian name for the fruit); the plant is a native of the West Indies where it is grown for its fruits; the *tuna* is, or was, an important article of food for the natives. They are red, ovalish or roughly egg-shaped and about 1½ inches across. The plant makes a shrub up to about 3 feet tall, with smallish flat joints, oval-shaped as a rule and about 4 inches long. The areoles are large, with yellow glochids and a few pale yellow spines. The flowers, 1½ inches across, are yellow tinged with red. *O. tuna* is one of several Opuntias that occasionally succeed out in the open garden – one could try it against a warm wall facing south, giving it a sandy soil and protecting it with suitable materials during a cold spell.

*O. tunicata* (*tunicate*, that is, covered or with a covering; referring to the spines). Borg mentions the synonoym *O. furiosa* (to make furious; madden) and says 'never was the name . . . more richly deserved.' The spines are the trouble: these are barbed, covered with a papery-white sheath and stick fast into the skin as soon as they are touched. This Opuntia however, is prized by growers and prospers in a pot in a sunny spot indoors. In its habitat, Central Mexico and the region from Ecuador to Northern Chile, it makes an erect bushy plant, about 18 inches tall, branched in whorls, and covered with long, sheathed spines. The joints or stems are small, almost round, glaucous green; they have prominent warts (tubercles), large white areoles furnished with pale yellow glochids and spines about 1½ inches long. The flowers, 2 inches across, are yellowish-green; and the fruits are small, pale green and spiny.

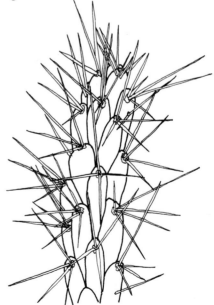

*Opuntia tunicata*

Our last species is *O. Vaseyi* (in honour of Dr. George Vasey or his son George Richard Vasey, the American botanists.) This species has egg-shaped joints, 4 to 5 inches long, thick and fleshy, pale green with an attractive bloom. The areoles, brown and prominent, bear usually one to three spines, about $\frac{3}{4}$-inch long, brown in colour and paler at the tips. The flowers are a striking shade of salmon-red and the fruits, 2 inches long, are deep purple. Collectors recommend it as being one of the easy Opuntias for growing in a pot indoors. The dozen or so described above are just as easy and all wonderfully decorative.

There *are* many, however, that are difficult, especially under cultivation in an ordinary living-room; these belong to what is known as the TEPHROCACTUS Sub-genus or Section (see page 76), and are seldom listed in nurserymen's catalogues. One which everybody would like to get hold of, I am sure, is *O. Bruchii*, with deep blue flowers – a native of Argentina. But I have never come across anybody who has grown it. Blue is a very rare colour in the cactus world.

The Opuntias I have described all require a winter temperature of not less than 50F (10C) plenty of sun and frequent watering during the growing season. In hot summer weather they should be stood outside in the open garden and sprayed once a week, with rain water if possible: tap water is not so good. And they prosper in a well-drained loam containing a fair amount of lime. You can, however, make up a compost such as the following, recommended by a firm of cactus specialists: two parts of sandy loam, and one part each of old powdered cow manure, powdered brick, silver sand, and crushed lime rubble (such as you get from a demolished building site).

Re-potting is only necessary after some years, and the strongest-growing plants are of course the ones that always need plenty of root room, for instance, *Opuntia robusta* (see page 81); and use the next-sized pot: thus a 6inch pot will follow a 5inch, and so on. You can tell when a change is necessary: the plant ceases to make new growth and the soil turns sour, often a green crust, resembling lichen, appearing on the surface. April is the best month for re-potting. Let the new soil become quite dry each time before you water; in this way the roots will be stimulated to vigorous growth and subsequently fill the pot. Then keep the soil moist all through the summer months. In the winter water just to prevent the joints from shrivelling. Once in six weeks will usually be enough.

Propagation of Opuntias is mostly from seeds (of the strong-growing kinds) or by cuttings. Hard seeds will germinate more quickly if soaked in warm water (rain if you can get it) for two days before sowing. Fresh seed germinates more quickly. Sow during warm summer weather in a temperature of 65–70F (19–22C) in pans of compost.

Cover with a sprinkling of brick dust and keep moist (not wet!) Cover with glass and shade with paper until the seedlings appear. If the seedlings look healthy they can be kept in the pan for a year but if they show signs of damping off they should be pricked out immediately into pans or pots.

*Opuntia grandiflora*

Seeds can be obtained from most specialist seedsmen and nurseries.

Two rare Opuntias raised from seed by an amateur were *O. grandiflora* and *O. Kleiniae*. The first (*large-flowered*) is a native of Eastern Texas and, according to the grower, has spineless, apple-green pads about 4 inches long, with golden-yellow glochids, and large deep yellow flowers, 4 inches across, streaked with red at the centre. ('Pads' is a good name for the joints or stems, which are flat and ovalish in shape). The plant grows well and flowers freely in a 3inch pot. It blooms in spring and early summer and is one of the tougher species that has succeeded in the open in favourable districts.

*O. Kleiniae* (probably in honour of J. Th. Klein, 1685–1759, a German botanist); an Opuntia with slender cylindrical stems, about 4 inches long and $\frac{1}{2}$-inch thick, branching from the main stem, which is $1\frac{1}{2}$ inches in diameter; the plant makes an erect bush some 4 feet tall. The prominent spines are about 2 inches long, and there are smaller ones on the older joints. The flowers are small and an uncommonly attractive shade of purple. Apparently an easy-growing species and, according to one gardener who grew it, it needs a fairly rich soil and plenty of water all through the summer months. The tips of the long slender stems were nipped by the frost during a particularly severe winter, but recovered and began rebranching the following spring. *O. Kleiniae* is a native of Mexico.

Seeds often take many years to produce sizable plants. Cuttings are preferred by most people, and furthermore they know what plants they are going to get. Mixed seed obviously can provide lots of surprises: some plants good, some occasionally worthless. The method used is to detach pieces of stem of almost any size and put them in a sunny place till a film or protective skin forms over the cuts. They are then inserted round the edge of pots filled with sandy soil (2 parts silver sand to one part of light loam); these are placed on a sunny shelf and water is given only when the soil has become quite dry. Subsequently and finally you keep the soil moist till the cuttings have rooted – you may have to wait six months. Cuttings can be taken at any time but the best time by far is late spring. Many gardeners today prefer to dip their cuttings in a hormone rooting powder.

Grafting is usually left to experts and, says a nurseryman, to professional gardeners who are out to produce curiosities. These curious plants are often exhibited at shows; they are usually grotesque – oddities that don't appeal to everybody. You take two dissimilar forms and graft them together. Late spring is the best time, when growth is beginning and the sap is on the move. Cut the stock straight across the top and notch it in the centre; this notch-shape is to take the wedge-shaped base of the scion; they fit together evenly and are pinned in place with spines of *Pereskia aculeata*.

Most cactus-lovers would like to have a show of cacti in their gardens; and several kinds have been recommended as suitable. Even in Britain some of the toughest have come through the winter undamaged by the weather – unscathed by frosts and winds. But they all grew in sheltered places, planted close to walls shielding them from the cold winds, and were always carefully covered up when a frost seemed imminent. I suppose that given plenty of care and attention the toughest sorts can be grown in quite cold districts. Among the species recommended are *Opuntia fragilis*, a wellknown and an invading plant. It is not fragile: *fragilis* means brittle and refers to the joints or pads, which break off at the slighest touch; it is a low, spreading shrub. Others are

*O. polyacantha*, said to be very hardy, and *O. tuna*, a shrub described on page 82. And see the list in the following Chapter, page 120.

The ideal position for them is against the sheltering wall of a greenhouse – if it is heated, so much the better. Preparation of the site is important. Excavate the soil to a depth of two feet; put in a 12inch drainage layer of broken bricks; cover it with a layer of turves – soil uppermost – and then fill up with the compost used for the potted plants (see page 84). I have used Yuccas as companion plants for cacti growing in a border;[1] but mostly pieces of rock are stood among them and the surface of the soil is covered with a layer of stone chippings to keep the roots cool and moist and give a touch of those desert places where the plants grow naturally.

Opuntias have been in cultivation longer than any other cacti and the generic name was mentioned as far back as 1588 – by the botanist Tabernaemontanus. Some writers state that the name is derived from Opus, a city in Greece, where the plants were cultivated. Others that the Indian Fig was 'a *native* of the country of the Opuntiani, whose chief town was Opus, in the vicinity of Phocis . . .';[2] this is incorrect, for the Opuntia is not indigenous to any part of Europe. According to one dictionary: '*Opuntia* (the name, originally given by Tournefort, is from a town in Greece where cactus-like plants are said to have grown).' Tournefort (1656–1708) was Professor of Medicine at the Jardins des Plantes in Paris. And the cactus-like plants were probably some sort of thistle.

*Pereskia aculeata*: this is the cactus that produces leaves (evergreen); and it belongs to the PERESKIEAE TRIBE or Group, the smallest Tribe,[2] comprising 19 species, and of these about six are described by botanists. And our plant is the one that appears in catalogues. Though why it does is perhaps something of a puzzle; for it is the least ornamental of all cacti and is only really decorative when in bloom; and to get it to bloom, you need plenty of heat – the winter temperature should not fall below 55F (13C). It is best grown in a greenhouse, and better grown in a greenhouse border, where it can develop easily and mature, than in a pot. Its flowers are its great attraction: they are roundish, many-petalled, white, pale yellow or pinkish, about $1\frac{1}{2}$ inches broad and come in clusters and are strongly scented. *P. aculeata* (*armed with spines*) is found wild in the region extending from Florida to the West Indies, Mexico and Argentina. It is a tall, climbing shrub in nature, with areoles in the axils of the leaves, bearing short hooked spines; the old stems are furnished with long, straight dark brown spines. (The presence of areoles is an obvious sign that the *Pereskia* is a cactus; when not in flower, it looks like an ordinary plant). The leaves are oval, from 2 to 5 inches long, pointed and short-stalked. The fruits are

87

[1]See page 10, Chapter 1.
[2]See page 10.

large, yellow, spiny and oval-shaped. The popular name of the plant is Barbados Gooseberry or West Indian Gooseberry. The fruit is excellent and is grown in large quantities in the West Indies. And the leaves are said to make a delicious vegetable.

Pereskias are the least finicking of all the cacti we grow indoors – unless, as I have already mentioned, we want them to flower freely. Plant them in any ordinary loam – take a potful from the kitchen-garden. They seem to survive plenty of neglect. Planted out in a bed in a greenhouse they can be left undisturbed for many years. Whether in pots or in beds, keep them dry throughout the winter, giving only enough water to prevent the leaves from shrivelling. If you want to increase your stock, take cuttings in late spring. Use small side shoots; remove the lower leaves and make a cut below the lower joint. Insert the cuttings in pots of sandy soil and put in a fairly sunny spot in a greenhouse till the roots form.

The generic name *Pereskia* (sometimes written *Peireskia*) commemorates Nicholos Claude Fabry de Peiresc (1580–1637) French naturalist and archaeologist.

# Chapter Four
# A Final Selection

*Pereskia aculeata* is more in demand as a stock for grafting than as a decorative pot plant.[1] And it is probably offered by nurseries principally for that purpose. I have never yet come across it in any florist's. It is often possible, however, to buy from a florist various cacti that are not always obtainable direct from the nurserymen. And the reason for this is that nursery stocks are sometimes down. The scarcity may be only temporary; on the other hand one may have to wait several years before the plants come into the market again. None of the following is listed in any of the current catalogues I have. *Lobivia* is a common-enough genus but according to several nurseries 'is in short supply at the moment'. Three different species were recently on sale, however, at one florist's I visited. (See page 93 for this genus).

Our first plant, *Ariocarpus Kotschoubeyanus*, from Central Mexico, was in the past something of a treasure. Three specimens were introduced into France about 1840 and one was sold in Paris for 200 dollars – a tiny plant only 1½-inches across. Literally worth more than its weight in gold. And a famous patron of horticulture, the Russian Prince Kotschubey – whom the plant commemorates – paid 1000 francs for a single specimen. Plants are now quite cheap. It is a gem and well worth trying to get. It will flourish for years in quite a small pot. A flat plant with overlapping triangular tubercles arranged in a rosette; they are covered with brownish wool and the pale purple flowers about an inch wide arise from the woolly centre at the top. *Ariocarpus* are normally spineless cacti. Although they prosper well in pots these must be deep because the plants have long, turnip-like roots. *Ariocarpus* come from sandy, stony regions, therefore in cultivation they need sandy, gritty soils – three parts sand, and one part each of powdered leafmould, garden loam, with a little rotted manure added.

*Bartschella Schumannii* (commemorating K. M. Schumann, 1851–1904, cacti specialist of the Botanical Museum, Berlin). A cactus very much like a *Mammillaria* (page 53) but with larger flowers. It is a rarity and regarded as quite difficult to grow successfully. Being a shallow-rooted plant it does better in a pan than a pot; it requires a really porous

[1] See pages 15 and 74.

soil and always a sunny position. This cactus is a native of Lower California where it makes large clumps of round or oval-shaped plant-bodies, these being grey-violet in colour and up to 4 inches high and about 2 inches thick. The tubercles are rounded, with areoles at their tips, which are at first woolly, then later naked. The tubercles are armed with spines, the smallest about $\frac{3}{8}$-inch long, the longest – the central one (one or two) – are white and tipped brown; the lowest is hooked and black. It is a curiously untidy-looking spiny plant but most attractive when in bloom; the flowers are purple with pale margins to the petals which form an open, star-shaped bloom $1\frac{1}{2}$ inches across. These flowers stand up well above the spines, at the top of the plant. A lot of people have remarked on the generic name *Bartschella* – a strange name for a Cactus. . . . The genus was named in honour of Dr. Paul Bartsch, Curator of the United States National Museum.

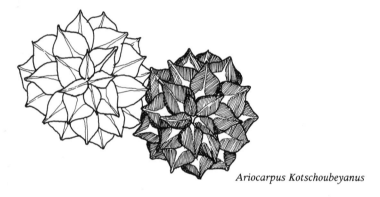

*Ariocarpus Kotschoubeyanus*

Cactus is the familiar name of all members of the family *Cactacaea* and most people use the word when they mention any sort they grow. *Cactus* is also a genus,[1] species of which are seldom offered by the nurseries. The only one I have ever come across is *Cactus intortus*, called by the florist who had it the Turk's Cap Cactus. This is the popular name of all the different species. There are about 30, natives of the West Indies and South America, where they grow within reach of the sea spray and many of them on barren rocks. It is impossible to reproduce the conditions under which they grow in their natural habitat. We can't, for instance, give them the sea spray and not a naturally saline soil, which they enjoy. The *Cactus* (that is, the species of this genus) are among the least amenable to pot culture; imported specimens don't live long; and those raised from seed take many years to grow into plants that bear any resemblance to those in nature.

[1] See page 1.

They never form the characteristic cephalium (head or cap). *Cactus intortus* (*twisted*) comes from the coastal regions of various islands in the West Indies. It is roundish and ribbed (up to 3 feet tall in the wild); the areoles are close together; and the spines which are yellowish, vary from ½-inch to 2 inches in length. The head or cap of white wool and brown bristles is tall and bears the pink flowers, which are about ½-inch long. This Turk's Cap Cactus makes a good contrasting shape to set with other cacti in a large pan. One of the latest introductions is the species with the remarkable name of *Cactus Broadwayi* – a curious combination of the ancient[1] and the modern. It is a native of Tobago Island (West Indies) and has a cylindrical plant-body with rounded ribs and small areoles furnished with short, horn-coloured spines. The cap is small: on fully-grown plants about 3 inches wide and an inch high; the flowers are also small and are purplish in colour.

*Bartschella Schumannii*

*C. salvador*, found in South America, is another (more beautiful) species with a similarly small cap or head and rosy-pink flowers. These cacti are favourite plants with South Americans, who mostly call the genus *Melocactus*; and to some of the Spanish-speaking communities the plants are known as *melones*. All the species and varieties transplant badly (as do many European Alpines) and are grafted or raised from seed. The best compost for them is made up of equal parts of gravel or sand and sifted leafmould. They need plenty of water throughout

91

[1] *Cactus* from the Greek KAKTOS, the name of an indigenous prickly plant which grew in ancient Greece; it wasn't however a Cactus; see also *Opuntia*, page 87.

the growing season, and should never be allowed to get dust-dry in autumn and winter. If you grow them, give them a sunny place in a window.

*Cochemiea Halei* (in honour of J. P. Hale, c. 1889, landowner in Lower California, and an enthusiast of cacti; the generic name is from the name of an Indian Tribe who inhabited Lower California where these cacti are found. Our plant comes from the Southern Islands and has slender stems 12 to 18 inches tall; they are covered with spines, the radial ones (10 to 20) are about ½-inch long; and the centrals (twice as long) come usually in clusters of 3 or 4. The tubercles are short, and the axils woolly. When in bloom this cactus is singularly attractive, with its smallish *Zygocactus*-like scarlet red flowers, which grow from the side axils round the top of the stems. I have seen it in bloom once in a private collection, an oldish plant which had formed clusters of tall stems; and along with it grew the species popular with American growers, viz. *Cochemiea Poselgeri*. The stems of a mature specimen reach a height of 6 feet but are seldom more than an inch thick. Those of the plant I am speaking of were half this size and a good blue-green. The tubercles, dark green (reddish in bright sunshine) are furnished with 7 to 9 short yellowish spines and a prominent central spine, hooked and about an inch long. The flowers are the same length, and a magnificent scarlet colour and grow from the axils of the top tubercles. Cochemieas need a warm, sunny position and a porous sandy soil. (Grafted plants are stronger than those raised from seed.) The soil must be kept moist all through the growing season; the best way to do this is to stand the plant in another receptacle containing tepid rainwater. *C. Poselgeri* commemorates Heinrich Poselger, d. 1883, a German Cactus-grower.

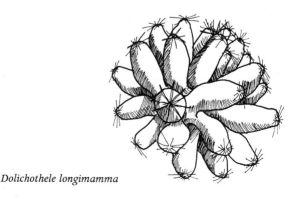

*Dolichothele longimamma*

*Dolichothele longimamma* like the other two species of this genus was formerly described under *Mammillaria*. (Dolichotheles differ from these plants in having much larger flowers). *D. longimamma* (*with long or large nipples – tubercles*), a native of Central Mexico, is perhaps the best known of the species. A fully-grown plant measures about 5 inches in height and the same in width. When about 3 years old it starts to bloom, the funnel-shaped, lemon-yellow flowers, measuring $2\frac{1}{2}$ inches across, appearing round the top of the plant. The tubercles are nearly 3 inches long, soft and fleshy and an attractive glossy green; they are furnished with inch-long, spreading spines (yellowish) and a shorter central spine with a dark tip. The plant does best in a semi-shady place indoors and needs a sandy loamy soil containing some lime. The generic name is from the Greek: *dolichos*, long; *thele*, a nipple; the specific epithet (see above) means the same and might therefore be thought to be redundant.

*Leuchtenbergia principis* has been frequently likened to an Aloe, a well-known succulent (see chapter 5, page 126). 'Another cactus, with a very uncactus-like name,' says a grower. . . . The genus (of one species only) is named in honour of Eugene de Bauharnis, Duke of Leuchtenberg, d. 1824, a French soldier and statesman. The plant is a native of Central and Northern Mexico and a favourite cactus with collectors (when they can get it) on account of its unusual shape and its singularly beautiful flowers, the latter being bright yellow and of a silky texture and measuring, when fully open, $3\frac{1}{2}$ inches across; they are also deliciously scented. The tubercles are very long, up to 5 inches, and do resemble the succulent leaves of some aloes. They are grey-green, three-angled and have woolly areoles at their tips; from them grow flat, papery spines, some about 4 inches in length. The flowers are borne at the tips of young tubercles. Not a difficult cactus to grow. As it has a long, tapering root, it needs a deep pot. A porous loamy soil containing some lime suits it best, and a sunny position. *L. principis* (*first, original*) is often reproduced by rooting the tubercles; though mostly it is raised from seed; the new plants flower after 4 or 5 years growth under glass.

*Lobivia* is a comparatively large genus; several species appear in catalogues but all, I find, under synonyms; for instance, *Echinopsis aurea*, which correctly is *Lobivia aurea*; and there are others (see page for *Echinopsis*).

First the name *Lobivia*: it is an anagram (transposition of letters) of Bolivia, where these cacti are found. The plants are round or cylindric in shape, the stems growing singly or in clusters; they are ribbed and usually very spiny. The flowers, which open in the day and close at night, are large, funnel-shaped and have short broad tubes.

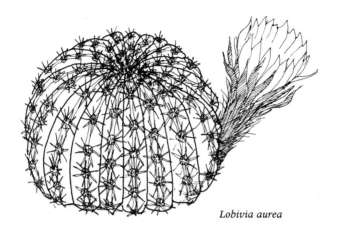

*Lobivia aurea*

*Lobivia chrysantha* (*with golden flowers*) is a native of Argentina, and common in the province of Salta bordering on Bolivia. Its flowers are its great charm; they are a pleasing shade of golden-yellow, with a purplish throat and very sweetly scented. The single stem, round and 2 inches tall, is a dull grey-green; on the ribs (13) the areoles bear only radial spines, (there are no centrals), red in colour at first, then later greyish. *L. chrysantha* is said to be the most floriferous of all the Lobivias in cultivation.

*L. cinnabarina* (*cinnabar-red; vermilion*) was described by botanists as long ago as the middle of the last century. It is prized by cactus-growers for the reddish-brown colouring of its flowers and for its quick growth; it is easily raised from seed. The stem is round, slightly depressed and later branches from the base; the ribs (18 to 20) are divided into sharp tubercles; and the areoles bear slender spines which are curved backward and grey in colour. This cactus makes an excellent pot-plant, the flowers lasting in bloom for several days. It is found high up in the Andes.

*L. famatimensis* is a species from La Rioja in Northern Argentina and famous for its many lovely varieties. It grows at altitudes from 6–9000 feet in the Sierra Famatima (sierra is a long, jagged mountain-chain). The colouring of the plant-stem is singular – dull green tinged with red. The flowers are unusually long: up to 12 inches, and funnel- or bell-shaped and bright yellow with a green throat. Like those of the other species they grow from the top of the stem. Our species is small and produces either a single stem or clusters. The stems have about 20 ribs, covered with white or pale yellow, short spines. The variety *albiflora* is singled out by collectors as the most striking (the specific epithet is something of a misnomer, since the flowers are occasionally a decidedly yellow). The white flowers are very beautiful – streaked with pale green in the throat – an uncommon colouring in Lobivias. In Var. *setosa* they are much less arresting, the colour being a yellowish- or creamy-white. Var. *aurantiaca* is a rich golden-orange; Var. *haematantha*, blood red; and Var. *rosiflora*, rose-pink – all worth having and hunting for. They are easily raised from seed.

*Lobivia famatimensis*

*L. mistiensis* is found near the volcano Misti, in the region of Arequipa, Southern Peru. The plant-stem is usually single, roundish and with 25 to 30 ribs, with areoles bearing, when young, white wool; the spines, all radial (no centrals) are mostly curved upward, and are about 2 inches long. The plant itself is about 3 inches tall and 2 inches wide. The flowers, 3 inches long, are pinkish and marked with red.

*L. Nealeana* has been described as a cactus having magnificent flowers on an inferior-looking plant. It is a small plant with single stems which eventually become bare at the base. The areoles are small and almost bare; the spines very thin and reddish in colour. But the flowers are certainly very beautiful, opening widely and revealing to

A collection of succulents

Plate X *Kalanchoe beharensis*, a charming foliage plant for a pot indoors

Plate XI *Sempervivum tectorum*, a hardy and very pretty houseleek for the rockery

Plate XII *Yucca filimentosa*, a fine foliage plant for a large pot or for a warm sunny border

*Aloe brevifolia*, an excellent succulent for a pot

97

*Aloe variegata*

*Crassula falcata* bears attractive
heads of scarlet flowers in summer  99

*Crassula lycopodioides*, a succulent
with scale-like leaves

*Sedum roseum*

*Sempervivums*

*Sempervivum kindingeri*

*Cheiridopsis    candidissima*    forms clumps of thick, fleshy leaves

*Crassula orbiculata*

*Echeveria*, Worfield wonder

*Gasteria verrucosa*, a beautiful succulent for a small pot

*Haworthia attenuata* with thick, fleshy leaves in rosettes

*Kalanchoe blossfeldiana*

*Stapelia variegata,* a succulent from
South Africa. A delightful plant for
a pot in a warm room

*Tradescantia zebrina*

111

advantage their lovely colour – a bright red with a metallic sheen. This *Lobivia* is much sought after for indoor decoration.

*L. Pentlandii* (in honour of Joseph Barclay Pentland, 1797–1873, who sent plants from Bolivia about 1838); it was the first species described and given at the time the name of *Echinopsis Pentlandii,* now a synonym. It has produced many attractive varieties, but not all flower readily. The type, however, is a reliable plant, carrying its funnel-shaped flowers on the sides of the stems; they are about $2\frac{1}{2}$ inches long and almost as wide, and a lovely glowing shade of orange-red. The stem is dark green, round or cylindric and slightly depressed at the apex; in time the plant forms large clumps and gives a fine display of flowers. There are 12 ribs, with prominent tubercles; the radial spines come from the margins of the areoles; they are yellowish and curved backward; the central spine, when present is longer and usually of a brownish colour. Botanists have listed at least a dozen different varieties; of these I have seen about half. Var. *Maximiliana* is in my opinion the loveliest, with its longer, pale green stem, its longer spines, and its exquisite flowers, rather differently shaped, and of a deeper carmine colour. In Var. *ferox*, the spines are long and curved. Var. *ochroleuca* has straw-coloured spines and yellow or deep orange flowers. Two which stood next to each other in their pots and in full bloom were Var. *albiflora* (not white-flowered however: the flowers were a shade of primrose-yellow); and Var. *rosea*, pale pink. They looked particularly attractive together.

*L. pugionacantha* (*with dagger-shaped spines*) is a rare species and is found at high altitudes (10,000 feet) in the mountains of Bolivia. It is a small plant and an exceptionally slow-grower. The stems, dull greyish-green, about $1\frac{1}{2}$ inches in diameter, are single or grow into clumps and have sharply-angled ribs. The spines are thickened at the base, and the flowers are yellowish-green and woolly on the outside – a favourite species with collectors who like to grow it in association with some of the furry-leaved high Alpines of Europe.

Lobivias need a mixture of equal parts of garden loam and sifted leafmould, with a little gravel and crushed lime-rubble added. The plants must be kept dry and on the cool side during the winter months.

*Monvillea Spegazzinii* (the specific epithet commemorates the Italian botanist, Professor Carlo Spegazzini, 1858–1926, who emigrated in 1879 to the Argentine and did much valuable research work there). Monvilleas are characterised by the long slender stems more or less prostrate; the nocturnal flowers, with very slender tubes, which remain attached to the fruits on fading; and the fruits, spineless, smooth and red. Our plant is a native of Argentina where, in the wild, the stems (under an inch thick) grow very tall; they are branched and

112

of a charming bluish-green, marbled white. The spines are about
¼-inch long and black. *Monvillea Spegazzinii* blooms freely, giving
two shows of flowers in early summer; the outer petals are pale pink,
the inner ones creamy-white; the length of the individual flower is
about 5 inches. An easy-to-grow cactus and one that makes rapid
growth. The genus is named in honour of M. Monville, a famous
student of cacti.

*Monvillea Spegazzinii*

*Neolloydia Beguinii* (commemorating l'abbé Beguin, born in 1886,
who collected cacti in the East Indies); this species is a native of Mexico
and among the best of the small cacti noted for their beautiful spines;
these indeed vie with the beauty of the flowers. The stem is cylindric,
4 or 5 inches tall, pale bluish-green in colour and entirely covered with
spines; most of these are ½-inch long, white tipped with black and very
sharp-pointed; there are also shorter ones, glassy white, and a long
central white spine. The flowers, 1½ inches long, which grow at the
top of the plant, are a charming violet-pink. The generic name *Neo-*

*lloydia* honours Professor Francis E. Lloyd, a collector of cacti – *Neo* was used because a genus of Alpine bulbous plants had already been named *Lloydia* (about 1700).

*Neoporteria nidus* (*nest-like*, referring to the bristly, hairy texture of the plant); a native of North Chile and reputed to be one of the more difficult cacti in cultivation. Grafted plants are stronger and better than imported seedlings. The glaucous stem (3 inches tall) is roundish, ribbed and completely covered with long white bristly spines curving upward; the stem becomes more cylindric with age. The areoles are densely set on the ribs and bear dark wool. The flowers are about $1\frac{1}{2}$ inches long, reddish in colour, with narrow petals, and arise from the crown of the plant. A remarkably attractive cactus on account of the bristly white spines which seem to form a protective (nest-like) covering to the plant-stem. Those who are able to buy a plant should try to get a grafted specimen. Neoporterias need a fairly rich soil, porous and sandy – equal parts of a lightish garden loam, grit and sifted leafmould; and they like plenty of sun and should be kept reasonably dry even during the growing season.

*Rhipsalis* are usually in short supply, a nurseryman tells me, for the simple reason that the Christmas Cactus (*Zygocactus truncatus*), a similar type of cactus (see page 73), is a much better plant in every way; in fact the beauties and virtues of this plant have eclipsed all the virtues of the *Rhipsalis* species together – there are about 60.

*Rhipsalis* aren't difficult to grow and the pendent interlacing stems or branches are shown to perfection when the plants are grown like the *Zygocactus* in hanging-baskets or (another method) attached by wire to specially prepared pieces of tree-bark.

The word *Rhipsalis* is from the Greek *rhips,* wickerwork, in reference to the pliability of the interlacing stems of some kinds. There are two popular names – Mistletoe Cactus, so-called because the fruits or berries resemble those of the common Mistletoe, though some *Rhipsalis* berries are pinkish in colour; Coral Cactus, the second name, is perhaps not so appropriate: the branching habit of the cylindric stems of some species do superficially resemble coral growing in the sea; but the stems of others, *Rhipsalis pachyptera,* for instance, are flattened and rather leaf-like.

They are epiphytic plants, like the Christmas Cactus, and occur in regions ranging from Florida and the West Indies, through parts of Mexico and down to Argentina. One or two species, however, are found in the Old World, in parts of Tropical Africa, and also in Ceylon and Madagascar. This fact always comes in for comment (see page 1); but botanists are of the opinion that these species are not indigenous plants and that seeds were originally carried by migratory birds or possibly by winds or currents of the sea.

   *R. Cassutha* is one of these species: it is a native of Florida and found in regions from there down to Southern Brazil, and also in Tropical Africa and Ceylon. This *Rhipsalis* produces very long pale green cord-like stems and forms an attractive hanging bush. These stems are cylindric and sometimes carry aerial roots; the joints are usually from 4 to 8 inches long and seldom more than $\frac{1}{4}$-inch thick. The areoles are small and bear when young very short bristles (in *Rhipsalis* spines are never strongly developed). The flowers, cream-coloured and small, grow singly from the areoles along the joints, and the berries, about $\frac{1}{4}$-inch wide, are white or rosy-pink. The specific epithet is sometimes mis-spelt Cassytha: *Cassutha* is correct.

*Rhipsalis grandiflora*

   *R. grandiflora* is a native of Eastern Brazil, in the region of Rio de Janeiro, and ultimately makes an upright much-branched bush nearly 4 feet tall. The flowers, as in all *Rhipsalis*, are not particularly large (*grandiflora*), about $\frac{3}{4}$-inch across and greenish-white in colour. This species is usually grafted on *Hylocereus undatus*, and then makes a much better plant – a fine ornamental for a large pot in a sunny but cool conservatory. The joints, like those of the preceding species, are cylindric; they are an attractive reddish colour when young, the longest measuring about 7 inches or so.

*R. mesembryanthemoides* comes from the same region as the above species and appears to be a favourite with amateur growers. It forms a pleasing pale green 18 inch-tall bush, the main stems of which have smaller stubby side ones densely packed together, resembling the succulent leaves of a *Mesembryanthemum*. But the flowers are nothing near so showy as those of the *Mesembryanthemums*: they are small and yellowish-white; none more than about $\frac{1}{2}$-inch wide. The fruits are round and white.

*R. pachyptera* (Greek: *pachys,* thick; and *pteron,* wing, referring to the flat, leaf-like joints of the stem); a native of Eastern Brazil, some plants growing at sea level, others high up in the mountains. This is one of the species with flattened stems; another is *R. elliptica*. These are very different in appearance from those with cylindric stems. Our plant makes an erect branched bush up to 4 feet high; the dark green flat pendulous stems are jointed, the smallest joints being about 3 inches long by 2 inches wide, with their margins notched and often coloured a charming purple-red. The flowers come on the marginal areoles, sometimes singly, sometimes in clusters of two or more; they are small ($\frac{3}{4}$-inch long), yellow tipped with red; the fruits are red and the size of a red currant. The areoles are woolly but lack spines. This plant, like most *Rhipsalis*, is usually grown in a hanging-basket so that the pendent stems can best display their graceful charm; true, the *Rhipsalis* are not particularly striking in bloom but they can provide a delightful lacy-looking background to some of the round or the columnar cacti when these are flowering at any time of the year.

As *Rhipsalis* grow in moist shady places in their natural habitat they need similar conditions, or something approaching them, in cultivation. It is not difficult to provide the shade (pulling blinds – indoors or in a greenhouse – or choosing an aspect shielded from the sun); but moisture in the air (humidity) can be provided only by frequent spraying with tepid rainwater (or sun-warmed tap water – left in the hot sun all day); the plants will benefit by an almost daily spraying during the summer months. Their natural soil is vegetable matter in the form of debris washed down the trunks of trees into clefts and holes where the plants are growing. In cultivation *Rhipsalis* need a fairly acid compost, say, equal parts of sifted peat or leafmould, powdered old cow manure and sandy garden loam. But it must not be too acid or rich or the plants will soon begin to deteriorate; a surfeit of leafmould, for instance, will eventually cause root rot and damping off; and this holds good for all kinds of cacti, even those for which rich composts have been recommended.

*Schlumbergera Russelliana*

*Schlumbergera* is a genus of two species and both are usually included by botanists in the Christmas Cactus Group. They are similar in habit to the Christmas Cactus (*Zygocactus truncatus*), but neither blooms till the New Year. *Schlumbergera Russelliana* is the first, opening its buds early in February. But the other, *S. Gaertneri,* doesn't begin to show any colour till March or later. And neither of these hanging or pendent cacti is as attractive or as popular as the Christmas Cactus. They don't appear in many catalogues nowadays; but they are worth trying to get, for they bloom at a time when flowers are scarce. Both species are epiphytes and can be grown like *Zygocactus* and *Rhipsalis*, in hanging-baskets; the soil those cacti need is also suitable for Schlumbergeras.

*S. Gaertneri* (named in honour of J. Gärtner, 1732–91, physician, of Stuttgart), a native of South Brazil, in the region of Santa Catharina, is the later flowerer of the two species; in fact, it is sometimes called the Easter Cactus. Like the other species, it is distinguished from *Zygocactus* in having regular flowers[1] with a short straight tube and four-angled fruits. The stems are spreading and pendent, green, with flattened joints truncated at the top, and varying in length from $1\frac{1}{2}$ to $2\frac{1}{2}$ inches, and are about an inch wide; they are notched with areoles on the notches, bearing one or two bristles; the flowers, bright red and star-

[1] Regular: uniform and symmetrical: the flower can be divided into two similar halves along any line passing through its centre.

shaped, measure 2 inches across and come freely even on young plants, usually at the tips of the branches. This cactus thrives best in cultivation as a grafted plant.

S. *Russelliana* (in honour of John Russell, 1766–1839, 6th Duke of Bedford, one of England's most enthusiastic botanists and gardeners); the plant is a native of Eastern Brazil and is sometimes called the Candlemas Cactus (Candlemas is held on February 2nd); the plant is in full bloom about that time. The stems are pendent or erect; the thin flat joints are ovalish, smaller than those of the other species: about an inch long and half-an-inch wide; they are notched on the sides, with one or two bristles in the areoles. The flowers, 2 inches or more long, are reddish-purple and come at the tips of the terminal joints. This *Schlumbergera* is very rare in cultivation; I have seen it only in botanical collections. The generic name commemorates Frederick Schlumberger, Belgian horticulturist, *c.* 1900.

A NOTE ON CULTIVATION

The best way to grow cacti (as it is for all plants) is out in the open air but this of course is possible only where the climate is suitable. In the Mediterranean regions many will grow well and live through winters which aren't too severe. Most of them, it must be remembered, need a winter temperature round about 45F (7C); for some, however – the epiphytic kinds, for instance – it should not be lower than 60F (16C). *Cactus intortus* (see page 90) need a winter temperature around 70F (21C). But these plants, especially, would be difficult to accommodate out of doors in places far removed from their native habitats.

Specialists who have experimented with outdoor cultivation in places such as Florida and Southern California advise cactus-lovers who are fortunate enough to live in these parts to choose a piece of ground sloping south or south-east and bounded at the top by tallish evergreens, say, in the form of a hedge, though not a hedge with long overhanging branches which would keep out the light and the sunshine – there are no plants that need so much. Better still would be a wall. And the district itself should not be far from the coast, so that the warm sea air and warm winds would soften any hard winter weather coming in from the hinterland.[1]

In Southern California, in regions on the Pacific seaboard, there are perfect sites for cactus-gardens and also in the Deep South: Florida (the 'Land of Flowers') is an ideal place.

In southern England cactus growers could try growing a few of the hardiest ones out of doors in parts of Cornwall and Devon and in other warm maritime districts but with the important addition of a wholly reliable overhead protective covering, such as strong plastic sheeting

[1]Some cacti indeed flourish most luxuriantly when constantly swept by sea breezes and also when the condition of the soil is slightly saline (see page 90).

to keep the plants warm and dry through spells of unexpected bad weather; and in damp weather the plants would need adequate ventilation, for damp does even more harm than cold. It would probably mean removing or lifting the plastic covering during a sunny break in the winter weather. In sub-tropical regions where the equable state of the temperature enables one to garden quite safely obviously no overhead protection is required.

The slope, wherever the garden is made, should not terminate at a pathway, but upon a low retaining-wall, one perhaps 12 inches or so tall. This wall will firstly keep the soil from the slope washing down on to the pathway and secondly will provide a good place to grow some of the cacti with hanging stems, the stems being trained over and down the face. The Christmas Cactus, along with *Rhipsalis* and *Schlumbergera* could be grown provided a shady spot could be found for them; on a slope facing due south this might be difficult; but one facing east should be shady enough after the morning sun has gone. Any trailing cacti may be grown along this ledge: our first-mentioned, viz. *Aporocactus flagelliformis,* the Rat's Tail Cactus, is certainly an excellent choice, since it is one of the easier cacti and revels in bright sunshine (see page 33).

It is important, of course, to choose the right soil for the cacti you are growing. This is particularly true of the plants that will be grown on a slope in sub-tropical countries; for these will be permanent and probably left undisturbed for many years.

In Britain cactus lovers can't hope to have much of a permanent collection in the open. Frosts are inevitable and no amount of protective material will save the more tender species.

One solution to the problem is to leave the plants in their pots and sink them in the soil. The tougher ones can be put out probably in late May (though May and even June in Britain are notoriously unreliable – killing frosts *do* occur – so protective cloches or bell-glasses should be kept ready in case they are needed); cover the rims of the pots with limestone chippings or pebbles of some sort and a sprinkling of silver sand. The plants will then bear the semblance of cacti growing in the wild. As soon as the weather turns cold they are easily lifted and housed till the following spring.

In the cactus gardens on the French and the Italian Rivieras and in the sub-tropics the soil is mostly of a character best suited to accommodate a wide variety of plants: a compost of lightish garden loam mixed with equal parts of coarse sand or grit and powdered lime-rubble is recommended. The cacti are planted firmly – the best time is late spring when the temperature is around 60F (16C) – and well watered in, preferably with rain water. Over the soil and particularly round the plants a layer of sifted leafmould or powdered peat is spread. This keeps the soil reasonably moist when it should be, that is, through the growing season and the hot summer days. Spraying is done regularly and of course carefully and wisely – some of the hairy species such as *Neoporteria nidus* (see page 114) and its variety *senilis* need to be kept rather dry even during the growing season. One must study the likes and dislikes of the different species and treat them accordingly. In late autumn, say, round about November, the layer of leafmould is scraped away so that the necessary drier soil conditions are obtained for the plants while they are in a quiescent state. Coarse sand, grit and cinders usually replace the leafmould and the peat.

The same conditions can be provided for the plants grown in warm southern regions of Britain and the same treatment given. For contrast, rocks and suitable plants are often set among the cacti and at the same time these provide a certain amount of shelter during bad weather. The succulents *Agave* and *Yucca* are eminently suitable for this purpose, their exotic-looking foliage according well with the diverse forms and varied colouring of the cacti, and the soil conditions suiting the Agaves and Yuccas admirably. Both these succulents are described in the second part of this book.

Opuntias, as I have already mentioned, are mostly recommended for growing outside in the open in Britain. And the best and most suitable are *Opuntia fragilis, O. humilis, O. opuntia, O. polyacantha, O. Rafinesquei;* these are among the hardiest (see page 86); even so they must be helped through severe winters by giving them plenty of protection. They like full sun, and a sandy slope facing due south is probably ideal for them. Other species such as *O. clavarioides, O. vesitia, O. floccosa, O. Spegazzinii* prosper only in semi-shady places.

The farther inland growers live in Britain and the farther north, the less likely are they to be able to grow any cacti at all in the open. At Kew Opuntias give a good show in a protected spot but are not spectacular. So most people in Britain have to grow cacti indoors – in a greenhouse or simply in a living-room. In a cool greenhouse, a great number can be readily accommodated, the requisite winter temperature of about 45F (7C) being maintained by the addition of a special oil-heater (usually necessary from December to March). Whether the plants are grown under glass or in an ordinary living-room, good ventilation and plenty of light are of paramount importance for their health and well-being. (See also Section 2, chapter 1, pages 11 to 13, on the subject of watering, etc.)

PESTS AND DISEASES

Often inadequate light is the cause of many cacti failing to grow into good healthy plants. It can prevent the flowers from opening, for instance, and also cause unnatural growth of the stems of some kinds, these running up and becoming weak and elongated. Again, rust-coloured patches on the plants are often caused by too much moisture in the atmosphere, which is due to inadequate ventilation.

Cacti are seldom attacked by fungus diseases. When these do occur the cause is over-watering and/or wrong soil conditions. The fungus *Phytophthora cactorum* will attack cacti seedlings growing in soil that has been kept too wet; to prevent this trouble, water with a suitable fungicide and always in moderation.

Although cacti are less susceptible to attack by pests than practically any other plants, insects of all kinds do find their way into indoor collections. They are often present in the soil used by growers – especially that taken from a kitchen-garden – and they may be introduced by other plants growing in the greenhouse or the living-room.

Ants, for instance, can be picked up in the soil which is to be used for re-potting. They damage the roots, loosening the soil to such an extent that the plants finally suffer from lack of moisture. Fortunately, these pests can be controlled by various insecticides. Ants, too, spread scale insects and Mealy Bug which cover the stems of cacti with a sooty mould and often do considerable damage.

Mealy Bug is one of the most destructive of all the pests which attack indoor plants. Its body, oval-shaped and somewhat flattened, is covered with a white mealy wax, which protects it from the toxic effects of any spray fluid. These insects are easily removed by hand from those cacti without spines, but not so easily from those with sharp spines and bristles. The best way then is to remove them with a pointed stick dipped in white oil emulsion or by painting them with a mixture of paraffin and methylated spirit, or a weak shellac varnish.

Scale insects are removed in the same way, though some growers prefer to wet the plant surfaces thoroughly first, and then apply a nicotine-soap spray forcefully, which soon kills these pests.

Red Spider Mite is another pest, very common in greenhouses, and very destructive to cacti and certain succulents such as Euphorbias and Mesembryanthemums (see chapter six, pages 177 to 179). These mites thrive in dry atmospheres and breed continuously through spring and summer. In a greenhouse it is possible to keep them down and ultimately get rid of them by frequent spraying, but this is not practicable of course in a living-room; there it will be necessary to dust the infested plants with finely powdered grade 16 naphthalene, this latter method also being used in the greenhouse if the mites persist after lengthy periods of spraying.

Thrips are minute black or dark brown insects (actually about one-

121

fifteenth of an inch in length) and attack stems and particularly flowers, causing them to grow distorted. To destroy these insects, dust the infested plants with grade 16 naphthalene (see above), or spray them with dilute nicotine-soap wash.

Aphis or Greenfly is seldom seen on cacti and succulents; but when the flies (aphides) do attack a plant they can be readily controlled by any reliable insecticide spray or dust. Root Aphis is more difficult to control. One of the symptoms of its presence in the soil is the failure of new growth to develop, and the pale unhealthy or etiolated look of the plant-stems. The infested plants may be lifted from their pots, the soil removed from the roots, which are then treated by washing them in an appropriate insecticide. A less drastic method – used when it is inadvisable to disturb the plant – is to immerse the plant in the insecticide.

One of the chief concerns of cactus-growers is getting their plants to flower freely and regularly – often they don't flower at all. 'Why don't my cacti bloom?' is a common query. Two main reasons are: a wrongly-balanced compost – too rich in nitrogen and deficient in phosphatic fertiliser; and too-high a temperature during the winter, which deprives the plants of their very necessary resting or recuperative period.

Two other matters connected with flowering – the flowers fail to open; the cause of this is that the temperature is too low and there is insufficient light; the treatment is simply to move the plants to a brighter, warmer, place in the room or the greenhouse. (Remember, though, that some cacti have flowers which do not open naturally – called cleistogamous flowers.) Flower-buds drop: again the temperature is too low for the plants, and they need more water; move the plants and spray them (as well as water them) more frequently.

Finally, put your plants outside in the open as often as you can; for there is no doubt that the fresh air, the summer sun, and warm rains do them the world of good.

# Chapter Five
# Succulents for the Garden

The Succulent plants we are dealing with in this part of the book are found in many parts of the world and occur for the most part in dry, open, situations where the soil is often starved and desert-dry. Like Cacti, they store up sufficient moisture to carry them through long spells of drought (see Chapter 1, page 11) and flourish and flower profusely under conditions that would prove fatal to most other plants. Given the right amount of care and attention, many tender Succulents will prosper in pots indoors and make a fine show for the home.

The vast majority are tender; unfortunately, very few are hardy enough for the garden: there are not more than about a dozen different genera containing hardy species; and from these we have to make our choice, remembering, too, that some are more tender than others. We take the plants alphabetically as we did the Cacti.

AGAVES are natives of the warm, southern parts of America – *Agave Parryi* is common in Arizona and New Mexico, where many cacti are found.

The genus belongs to the Family *Amaryllidaceae,* though the writer Walther Haage states that all the species – over 300 of them – are now placed in a family by themselves, viz. the Fam. *Agavaceae.*

Agave is derived from *agavos,* meaning admirable; referring to the showy appearance of the plants when in bloom.

There are apparently two popular names. One, extant, the *Century Plant;* the other, seldom heard nowadays, the *American Aloe,* seemed to be used only for *Agave Americana,* which is the best-known kind. (Aloes have a superficial resemblance to Agaves and *Agave Americana* I have heard called an aloe – a giant one – by people seeing it for the first time.) Agaves were called *Century Plants,* since it was the common belief that it took them 100 years to reach the flowering stage. But this is completely wrong, although many types growing in cool climates are notoriously slow in producing flowers; and those in pots often fail to bloom at all, at least in their owners' lifetime. Normally the smaller kinds bloom after about eight years; and only the larger kinds take 30 years or more to produce a flower-spike.

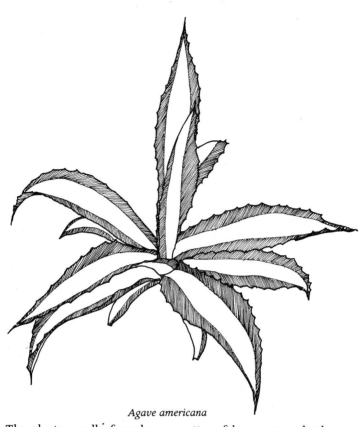

*Agave americana*

The plants usually form large rosettes of long narrow leathery or fleshy leaves, which end in a sharp spine (often as sharp as a needle) and are toothed. The flowering spikes arise from the centre of the rosettes and in some types are very tall – 20 feet or more. When they die the plants themselves usually die too; many, however, produce plenty of offsets, which are easily grown on for stock.

*A. americana* is a native of Mexico and is commonly seen in gardens along the Mediterranean, where it has become naturalised. It makes a very large rosette of grey-green leaves, which are from 3 to 6 feet long and 6 to 9 inches wide. The teeth are short and dark brown. The flowers, small and yellowish-green, come in dense clusters at the end of spikes often measuring 25 feet or more in height. A really striking exotic-looking, foliage plant, it is suitable for warm English gardens, and hardy enough for districts farther north, provided it is protected during bad winters; which means covering it over with some sort of frost-proof material, such as plastic-sheeting, when a sharp frost is imminent. In open weather, at least in the south of England, it needs no protection, and some really fine plants, mostly grown as single specimens, can be found there.

But more favoured by gardeners are the varieties of this *Agave,* viz. Var. *Marginata,* which has wavy-toothed margins, with widish yellow bands; in some plants these may be creamy-white in colour. Var. *Marginata Aura* has bright yellow or greenish-yellow stripes. There are others perhaps not so well known. They all make admirable companion plants for those Opuntias that can be grown in the garden (see page 86).

More striking and ornamental is the species *A. Franzosinii,* with bluer leaves; it is described as very similar to *A. americana* but some gardeners have found it not quite so hardy. It is well worth a trial in the south of England and is really remarkably decorative when its long bluish leaves extend out over a closely-mown grass path. Plant the *Agave* about a foot in from the edge of the path and be careful when you mow the grass that you cut round the outstretched leaves. The fresh green grass contrasts well with the bluish colour of this *Agave.*

Two other hardy species are *A. Parryi* and *A. utahensis.* The first-named dies after flowering but reproduces itself by the bulbils that form in the infloresence. *A. Parryi* is a smaller *Agave* than *A. Americana,* the leaves, thick and fleshy, being 10 inches long and 3 inches wide, dull grey-green (glaucous when young) and ending in a sharp strong black point an inch long. The leaf margins are set with small teeth, often hooked; and the flowers, creamy-white and 2 inches long, come in a panicle at the top of a stem often 12 foot tall. This species was named in honour of Dr. C. C. Parry, who introduced the plant to cultivation in 1868.

*A. utahensis* is another small species, with greyish leaves 12 inches long and 2 inches wide which end in a grey spine; the flowers come in a tall spike from 5 to 15 feet long. This species is a native of the Grand Canyon Region and common in Utah and Arizona. People who have grown it say it is not quite so hardy as *A. Parryi* and should have overhead protection during bad weather.

These hardy Agaves are naturalised in many hot countries such as Italy, Spain, Portugal and the West Indies and are used in gardens not only as ornamentals but as useful hedging plants.

*A. sisalana* is important economically, since it produces a fibre used for cordage – Sisal is the name of the port of Yuccatan from which most of the fibre is shipped. Apparently 1000 leaves produce about 70lbs. of fibre, which is largely used for rope making and for binder twine.

The garden varieties need a well-drained sandy loam – never heavy soil – and plenty of water during the summer months.

There are several species, on the small side, very suitable for growing in pots: *A. parviflora* is one of these. The plants are described at the end of Chapter Six, page

*Agave parviflora*

*Aloe aristata (having a beard or awn – bristle-like appendage; referring to the leaves)*; this is the only species listed in English catalogues of hardy perennial plants. I doubt very much though whether it would survive a severe winter in gardens around London without some protection. However, it is worth a trial. One catalogue describes it as 'a rare garden plant, a native of South Africa, where it thrives in poor sandy soil. It has thick dark green succulent leaves which store quantities of water during the rainy seasons; it is thus able to withstand long periods of drought . . . plant it in spring.'

Aloes may be stemless (as in our plant, *A. aristata*), or develop in time long stems, some being 20 feet or more in height. The leaves, toothed, fleshy and succulent, form rosettes, as do Agaves, but Aloes do not die after flowering.[1] *A. aristata* has numerous leaves (2 to 4 inches long and ½-inch wide) forming a dense rosette up to 8 inches

126

[1] The flowers of Aloes do not take the place of the growing points in the rosettes, as in the Agaves; but grow laterally from the axils of the leaves.

across; the leaves have slender white spines along the edges; they end in a long, thread-like or bristle-like appendage and are marked with white tubercles. The scape, or flowering stem, is 18 inches tall; the flowers, about 40 in number, are reddish-yellow and carried in a loose raceme. The plant is usually in full bloom during late July.

It is a difficult plant to accommodate in an English garden. It looks curiously artificial in the herbaceous border and might, I think, be best in a pocket, on its own, in the rockery. Perhaps a dozen plants set well to the front, at ground level, where they will get more moisture. They should be packed fairly close together so that no soil is visible. The rosettes, dark green and ornamented with pearly-white tubercles and bristles, are pleasing to look at before and after flowering time. The slender scapes, perhaps 20 or so in a clump, with their hanging reddish-yellow flowers, give a much richer effect than would just one or two. The plants should have a background of some good quality rockery-stone (facing west): it will show up the plants to best advantage and at the same time afford extra protection against severe frost. You can increase your stock by offsets which are freely produced as a rule by this species. As Aloes hybridise readily seeds are not recommended: you may get a strange mixture of plants, most of them inferior.

Another way of growing *A. aristata* is to use it as a permanent bedding-plant in a round bed, which should not be too big – not more than about 18 inches in diameter. You will need a good many plants and they should be set close together, beginning with the one in the centre and the others arranged in circles round it till the bed is filled. You can also have an edging of something suitable such as the Houseleek called *Sempervivum tectorum calcareum*, which has fleshy rosettes of glaucous-green leaves tipped purple; as it seldom flowers it makes a particularly good edging. The bed should be cut out in the middle of a small lawn which has a certain amount of shade on it during the hottest part of the day. Aloes do not thrive in the scorching sun. The well-known Partridge-breasted Aloe, *A. variegata,* is occasionally used as a bedding-out plant in warm gardens, but as it is intolerant of lime in the water it must always be sprayed and watered with rain-water. It is one of the tender species and consequently cannot be left outside in winter.

Aloes need a well-drained soil, consisting of a lightish garden loam with plenty of coarse sand and grit added. At the time of planting, a little sifted leafmould or peat should be put round the roots. (For the cultivation of the tender species grown in pots indoors, see the following chapter.)

There are about 200 different species, most of them natives of South Africa and the adjacent islands. Aloes belong to the Family *Liliaceae*;

and the genus *Aloe* formerly included many species now separated into *Haworthia; Gasteria;* and *Apicra*. The word *Aloe* is from *Alloeh,* the Arabic name for the plant. ('Bitter Aloes' is fairly frequently heard but not everybody knows what it is. Bitter Aloes is the dried bitter juice of the leaves of *Aloe vera,* used as a purgative and in various medicines. The plant is widely cultivated in the West Indies for this product.)

*Aloe variegata*

*Bulbine annua (annual)* is usually treated as an annual; seeds are sown in gentle heat in early March and the seedlings planted out as soon as they are big enough; they grow quickly and flower in June. *Bulbine* is a genus of about 25 species, most of which are natives of South Africa – two come from Eastern Australia. They are by no means common and not many nurseries have them; those that are occasionally offered are all tender and must be housed during the winter months. *B. annua* is from South Africa and needs a deep sandy loam and a sunny, sheltered position (it is possible to get seeds as a rule from leading seedsmen). It is about 9 inches tall, has fleshy, awl-shaped, rounded leaves and yellow flowers borne in a terminal raceme. An attractive little plant and more striking when grown in a clump against a sunny boulder in the rockery – a single specimen doesn't give much of a show. Try growing over the boulder the creeping *Veronica prostrata*, which has small deep blue flowers carried in short dense clusters – a charming association of yellow against a background of blue. Both plants bloom at the same time. You can, if you prefer a different colour scheme, use the pink-flowered variety *rosea* instead of the blue; or the light blue *Trehane*, which has pretty golden-yellow foliage; they bloom simultaneously with the *Bulbine*. The genus *Bulbine*, like the *Aloe*, belongs to the Lily Family (*Liliaceae*). And the generic name is from the Greek *bolbos*, a bulb: the plants have thick, fleshy rootstocks, often described by botanists as 'somewhat rhizomatous or bulb-like'.

*Chiastophyllum oppositifolium* is listed in most catalogues of hardy perennials and alpine plants and often the synonym *Cotyledon oppositifolium* appears with it; the plant is better known by this name or by the garden name of *Cotyledon simplicifolia*. One nursery describes it as 'An Alpine from the Caucasus, with succulent leaves and small golden-yellow flowers, borne in drooping racemes. A perfect plant for walls. Blooms from April to June – 6 inches, 20p per plant'.

The specific epithet *oppositifolium* refers to the leaves – *opposite to each other on each side of the stem;* and the generic name (also referring to the leaf-character) is derived from *kiastos,* decussate (at right angles); and *phyllon,* leaf. The leaves are fleshy, roundish in shape and coarsely toothed; they come in 3 or 4 pairs on the creeping stems, which, with the hanging and often branched racemes of tiny yellow flowers, make it an ideal plant for adorning a wall; the wall of course must be a dry, or retaining wall, built especially to accommodate plants in its crevices. This *Chiastophyllum* (the only species, by the way) needs a sunny position and a compost consisting of loamy soil, with which coarse sand and grit have been mixed.

As it blooms in spring, there will be no difficulty in finding other wall plants to grow with it. I suggest any of the paler-coloured Aubrietias, such as *Studland,* lavender; *Maurice Prichard,* pale rose-pink; and *Riverslea Pink,* another rose-pink. The richer-coloured varieties, such as *Dr. Mules* (a vivid purple) and *Crimson Queen,* are inclined to over-power the more modest-looking yellow *Chiastophyllum*. The plant is usually propagated by cuttings.

*Crassula sarcocaulis* is the only species (of about 300) that can be grown in English gardens without protection in winter. Like the *Chiastophyllum, Crassula* belong to the Family *Crassulaceae*. The generic name is from *crassus,* meaning *thick,* and refers to the thick, fleshy leaves – *sarcocaulis* means *fleshy stem*. This hardy shrubby *Crassula* is

9 inches tall and blooms in late summer, bearing pink flowers in open clusters; the flower-buds are bright red and show up well against the small, green, pointed leaves. An attractive plant for many months of the year and useful for growing in a pocket in the rockery (recommended by most gardeners) or for the front row of the herbaceous-border. Wherever it is planted, it looks more striking in a clump. It needs a sandy loamy soil, containing plenty of grit, and flowers more profusely in full sun. It is a native of South Africa and may be propagated by seeds, cuttings or leaf cuttings. A good companion for it is one of the dwarf late summer-blooming Aster Hybrids, such as Blue Bouquet (15 inches tall) or the smaller (6 inch) Little Blue Baby, with mid-blue flowers. Plant this succulent in spring so that it will be well established in the soil before the cold weather sets in.

*Mesembryanthemums* are found under various different names. So, one current catalogue lists *M. edule,* and another, *Carpobrotus edulis,* which is the same plant. A leading horticultural dictionary states that the latter genus is now included in *Mesembryanthemum;* and this is the name I have used here. *M. edule* (*edible;* referring to the fruit) has the popular name of Hottentot Fig. The plant is a native of Cape Province (South Africa) where it grows into a good-sized shrubby plant with long trailing stems, carrying succulent green leaves and yellow or purple daisy-like flowers, these being followed later in the year by big fleshy fruits. In Britain it doesn't give such a good show and may not survive the winter in many districts. It is best suited to the warm seaside gardens of the south coast and is well adapted for training over a low rock wall. This species has thick, 3-angled green leaves up to 5 inches long and flowers measuring 3 or 4 inches across. In autumn the whole plant turns red and makes an attractive show of colour till the frosts come.

*M. uncinatum* (*hooked at the end;* referring to the leaf-sheaths); this is also from Cape Province and like the other species does best in warm seaside gardens; both flower more freely, by the way, in soil which is not too rich. It should be a lightish loam mixed with plenty of sand and grit. These Mesembryanthemums need full sun and must be planted in spring. *M. uncinatum* has long prostrate stems; its leaves are grey-green in colour, and the flowers, anemone-like and small ($\frac{3}{4}$-inch across) are an exquisite shade of magenta-pink; they are usually at their best in early September. Both plants have become naturalised on the cliffs along the south coast of England.

The half-hardy annual kinds are often grown outside, the seeds being sown in April where the plants are to bloom. The famous and best known one is the Ice Plant, *M. crystallinum,* which has long succulent stems and fleshy leaves covered with glistening papillae (soft protuberances) and bears in summer small whitish, rather insignificant flowers. In the Mediterranean region and parts of California it grows freely as a wild plant on rocks and cliffs. This species is a native of South Africa and Arabia. Another is *M. tricolor* (*three-coloured*), from Cape Province; it has erect stems, grey-green leaves and aster-like flowers, pinkish-red and pale yellow in the centre.

*M. criniflorum* (Livingstone Daisy) a half-hardy annual, is 3 inches tall, and splendid for dry and sunny positions. It is a native of Cape Province and has short stems branched from the base; roughly cylindrical-shaped leaves and flowers $1\frac{1}{4}$ inches wide usually white tipped with pink. Plants raised from seed are often variously coloured, including pink, carmine, salmon, apricot and orange. Sow *Mesembryanthemum* seed thinly on the surface of the soil, rake in, and when the seedlings are big enough to handle set them out about 3 inches apart and water them till they are well established and begin to make good healthy growth. Propagate the hardy species by taking cuttings after the plants have finished flowering; but they may also be taken any time between March and September. If they are covered with a bell-glass they may even root outside in the garden. Select pieces 2 to 6 inches long, according to the size of the plants; remove some of the bottom leaves, then lay the cuttings on a shelf to allow a protecting skin to form over the cut part. (This is the prescribed method of preparing all cuttings of a succulent nature – see Chapter 3, page 86, where the propagation of Opuntias is described.) They are then inserted in pots of sandy soil, and the pots are placed on a shelf or put in a cold frame till roots are formed. The new plants are potted separately, first in 3 inch pots and then after a season or two in those of bigger size.

The tender, rarer, kinds of Mesembryanthemums, described in the following chapter, are grown in pots indoors – in the greenhouse or in those places where they are safe from frosts – they are more succulent than the so-called hardy and the annual kinds. These tender Mesembryanthemums are the choice ones prized by collectors; many of the plants are split up into different genera; see, for instance, *Cheiridopsis; Conophytum; Faucaria; Lithops; Pleiospilos,* Chapter 6. *Mesembryanthemum* and all these related genera belong to the Family *Aizoaceae*.

*Penthorum sedoides* (*sedum-like*) is a hardy succulent plant commonly known as the Virginian Stonecrop and recommended for growing in the water-garden. There are three species and this is the best known. It is an erect perennial, somewhat branched and about 2 feet tall; it has small, narrow, fleshy pale green leaves, which eventually turn bright orange, and clusters of pale greenish-yellow flowers, usually at their best in late summer. You need a good-sized clump to get a really good show; the colour is never very striking, however. The best way is to grow these Penthorums (say, a dozen or so) in shallow water, and on the bank of the pond or stream some water-loving contrasting plant such as *Astilbe chinensis pumila* (12 inches tall), with lilac-rose plume-like flowers in September, which is the time when the *Penthorum* is at its best. It needs a loamy-leafy soil (if grown in water, put stones round the crown of the plant till well rooted and established). Specimens obtained in pots may be set out in the garden at practically any time of the year. Seeds should be sown outside in March.

*P. sedoides* is a native of North America. The generic name is derived from *pente*, five; and *horos* a column; referring to the capsule (dry seedcase) which is 5-angled and 5-beaked). *Penthorum* belong to the Family *Saxifragaceae*.

*Portulaca* includes the Common Purslane, the young fleshy shoots of which are used in salads or for pickling. The specific name is *Portulaca oleracea;* and the specific epithet means *of the vegetable garden*. This species is usually treated as a hardy annual. *P. oleracea* grows 6 inches tall and is of spreading habit. It has small fleshy oblongish leaves and bears yellow flowers, often in clusters, in summer. It is not grown as an ornamental but solely for its edible shoots and leaves. The plant is a native of Southern Europe and is widely grown on the Continent for its use as a pot-herb. Altogether there are about 40 different species of *Portulaca;* they come from the warmer regions of the world and many are American.

The famous one is *P. grandiflora* (large-flowered), a native of Brazil, which needs a hot dry summer if it is to succeed in English gardens. It has produced numerous varieties, all showy plants that every gardener loves to see blooming in his flower border. The popular name is appropriately the Sun Plant. This *Portulaca* and its varieties are described in a seed-catalogue as 'half-hardy annuals of easy culture in light sandy soils and flourishing in a sunny situation. Brilliant flowers, rose, orange-scarlet, purple, yellow and white, in great profusion. 6 inches.' The illustration in the catalogue shows these colours and all the flowers appear to be double. The plants may be hybrids or perhaps varieties of *P. grandiflora flore-pleno* which has double flowers. They open and are at their best in full sun, and close in shade.

The type (*P. grandiflora*) has stems 4 to 5 inches long and somewhat fleshy cylindrical leaves; the flowers come at the tips of the stems in a cluster and are surrounded by whorls of leaves; they bloom in June and July. In the variety *aurea* the flowers are golden-yellow; in *rosea,* rose-pink. Var. *compacta* is of more compact habit than the type and has flowers of various colours. Var. *Regelii* is a more erect plant, with red-purple flowers, large and usually solitary; in many of the varieties

132

they come in clusters. The individual flowers measure an inch across and are of an exquisite satiny texture. One method of raising these Portulacas is to sow the seed under glass in March and plant out the seedlings in May. But they often fail to develop into strong healthy plants. The best way is to sow the seed in the place where the plants are to bloom. Sow thinly during May in a raised bed of light sandy soil in the hottest sunniest part of the garden – easy enough to find in a rockery facing due south – and sprinkle the seeds with a little sand and sifted leafmould; the plants thus raised will grow well and bloom freely about July. Thin out the seedlings to 6 inches apart, taking care not to disturb the roots of those you leave in place. Perhaps the rockery is the best place for these brilliant succulents. The raised open bed or pocket, prepared among rocks or boulders facing south, will catch all the sun available and help the plants to grow quickly and develop large healthy flower-buds.

The species *P. foliosa* (*full of leaves*), a native of Guinea, has very narrow succulent leaves, and yellow flowers, usually carried in clusters of 3, which are at their best in June.

The genus *Portulaca* belongs to the Family *Portulaceae;* and the generic name is from *Portilaca*, the name used by the Roman naturalist Pliny (AD 23–79).

Our last two genera containing hardy succulent plants both belong to the Family *Crassulaceae*. The *Sedums* are called Stonecrops and the *Sempervivums* Houseleeks.

*Sedum* is from the word *sedo*, to sit, in reference to the way in which some Sedums attach themselves to rocks and walls. There are at least two dozen different species and many varieties, enough in fact to furnish a small flower-border or a small rockery without including any other hardy succulents.

Perhaps the best known and most widely grown in British gardens are *Sedum spectabile* and *S. acre* (called the native Golden Stonecrop). *S. spectabile* (*spectacular; showy*) is erroneously called the Ice Plant (see the preface) – the popular name Ice Plant belongs to *Mesembryanthemum crystallinum*, described on page 130. *S. spectabile* is a native of China and is much valued for its flat showy flower-heads which are at their best in September; additional attractions are the Red Admiral Butterflies which settle on the flowers to collect honey. In deep rich soils, this Sedum grows up to 18 inches tall and produces thick, glaucous succulent stems and pale green cool-looking fleshy leaves, often 3 or 4 inches long and 3 inches wide. The tiny individual pink flowers which make up the flat-topped heads (corymbs) are $\frac{1}{2}$-inch wide. There are a couple of deeper coloured varieties, viz. Var. *atropurpureum*, with red-purple flowers; and Var. *roseum*, reddish-pink.

133

Both are more striking than the usual pink kind. In the herbaceous-border, plant these Sedums in bold clumps. You need at least three ot a clump for a really good show. These Sedums do surprisingly well, too, in town gardens, provided they are grown in soils that have been well dug over and enriched with powdered peat or leafmould; both materials may be obtained from any seedsman. Propagate *S. spectabile* and its varieties by division after flowering. Many gardeners prefer to winter the new plants thus obtained in a cold frame, and then set them out in April.

Sedums are also raised from seeds, these being usually sown in the place where the plants are to bloom. *S. acre,* the Golden Stonecrop, is native to Britain and forms mats of bright yellow flowers. It flourishes on dry walls or in the rock-garden. It is a hardy perennial, flowers in June–July. *S. acre* has also the popular name of Wallpepper and has a wide distribution: Britain to Persia (common in Southern Europe), and Norway to North Africa. British native plants are more commonly found in maritime districts than anywhere else. The bright shining golden-yellow flowers make this *Sedum* one of the showiest of the whole family, and a valuable garden plant: a cheerful patch of colour in the rockery when most of the other Alpines have finished blooming, and a real treasure for adorning sink and trough gardens. When in full bloom the plant makes a mat of spreading golden-yellow flowers (each flower about $\frac{1}{2}$-inch across), which completely covers the fleshy, conical, deep green leaves. These tiny evergreen leaves make an interesting cover for rock-work during the winter months, though for foliage effects some of the varieties give a more striking show. For late winter and early spring I single out the lovely *S. acre var. aureum,* which has its leaves tipped with bright golden-yellow – a choice plant for a wall garden when nothing is in flower. It likes a poor sandy soil and a sunny position – both easy enough to find on most dry, retaining walls. Another variety, with silver variegation instead of gold, is *elegans,* an attractive carpeter but unfortunately not quite so hardy as the golden variety. The smallest is Var. *minimus,* only about $\frac{1}{2}$-inch high; it is a neat, compact and attractive variety. An ideal plant for a miniature sink or trough garden. The finest of all, according to people who grow it, is Var. *majus,* which has larger flowers than the others, large pale green leaves and is a more robust plant; it is a native of the mountainous parts of Morocco and is sometimes listed in catalogues as *Sedum Maweanum.* I have seen specimens in full bloom in rockeries and I think gardeners are inclined to overprize it; its flowers are cer-tainly larger, much larger than those of the type, for instance; but they are much paler in colour and completely lack the sunshine brilliance of the smaller kinds. *S. acre* is easily increased by division; most of the creeping stems have roots. The specific epithet means *biting,* which refers to the acrid taste of the leaves; in the past the plant was used medicinally as an emetic (a medicine to cause vomiting) and a cathartic (purgative).

There are many other Sedums suitable for rockeries and wall gardens; they will creep over stones and down the face of a dry wall or make spreading mats of flowers and foliage to fill a pocket in the rock garden; and they may also be used for edging an ordinary flower border.

The annual and biennial kinds are sometimes more difficult to come by; most of them, however, are raised from seed, which is easy enough to get from any leading seedsmen. The tall-growing border Sedums are on the whole not so plentiful – as already mentioned, *S. spectabile* is by far the most common and popular.

*S. maximum,* found wild in many parts of Europe, has produced some fine border varieties; one of the best is *S. maximum atropurpureum,* described in the catalogues as 'A tall robust plant reaching a height of 2 or 3 feet in deep rich soils. Stem and leaves both purple-red. Large flower-heads a deep pink. August to September.' The leaves often measure 5 inches in length and sometimes come in threes. (The meaning of *maximum* is *largest;* and *atropurpureum, dark purple.*)

*S. telephium* is another British native species popularly known as *Orpine* and also as *Live for ever.* It is a succulent herbaceous fleshy-leaved purple-flowered plant common in English cottage gardens. The varieties it has produced are much more striking; the finest is Var. Munstead Red, a plant up to 2 feet tall, with ovalish leaves 3 inches long and $1\frac{1}{2}$ inches wide; the flowers, carried in large, spreading clusters, are deep dusky red and at their best usually at the end of August. In the variety Variegatum the leaves are attractively marked with cream and white. The specific epithet is something of a puzzle; one explanation is that it is possibly connected with Telephus, a king of Mysia in Asia Minor.

The prettiest of the annual kinds is *S. coeruleum* (*blue;* referring to the flowers). It is the only blue-flowered Sedum and the only annual kind worth growing in the garden. This species is a native of Southern Europe and North Africa. It is a dwarf, branched plant, with stems 3 inches or more high and small leaves (about $\frac{1}{2}$-inch long), both turning bright red when it is grown in poorish, sandy soils and in full sun. The flowers, star-shaped, are pale blue, each one $\frac{1}{4}$-inch across, and are carried in loose clusters; they bloom in July and August, at a time when colour in the rockery is rather scarce. *S. coeruleum* is delicate-looking, but is hardy enough for gardens and easily raised from seed. Sow it thinly in early April where the plants are to bloom. In warm sheltered places, say, in a sunny pocket in the rock-garden, the plant will sow itself. Dry hot places help to produce those really red stems and leaves which contrast so strikingly with the pale blue flowers.

There are at least another couple of dozen dwarf Sedums suitable for rock-gardens and many of them charming enough to grow in pots in a cool room or a cold greenhouse. *S. dasyphyllum* (*shaggy-leaved*) is one. It is described in a current catalogue as 'A hardy species, suitable for growing in a pot or on a rockery. If grown indoors in winter, a little water is necessary at all times.' Some specimens are more shaggy (hairy) than others. It has tiny greyish leaves and small heads of pinkish flowers on spreading, branching stems about 2 inches tall. A light, sandy soil which is warmed by the sun keeps the plant nice and compact. It blooms about the middle of June and looks delightful partly hanging over a ledge at the top of a dry wall. As portions of the stems easily become detached and root in the soil plenty of new plants are always available. This species is widely distributed on the continent of Europe – more common in southern regions – and extends to parts of North Africa.

*S. pilosum* (*covered with long, soft hairs*) is one of the biennial[1] Stonecrops. We sow the seed in spring and let the plants develop (after thinning-out) where they are to flower the second year. The first year this Sedum, with its rosette of small dark green hairy leaves, much resembles a Houseleek (*Sempervivum*). In the second year in May and June, it sends up 4 inch stems with heads of attractive rose-pink flowers (about 3 inches across) rather like those of *Crassula falcata*. It is a fine Sedum for the rockery or a low crevice in the wall garden. It comes from the mountainous regions of Persia, the Caucasus and Asia Minor.

*S. Sieboldii* is one of those species variously described as 'quite hardy', 'hardy in many districts', 'tender' and 'suitable only for pots'. It is certainly hardy enough for rockeries in the south of England, and where it will survive the winter if given some overhead protection. It is, however, much favoured as a pot-plant, principally on account of its hanging, arching stems (6 to 9 inches long) with their beautiful bluish succulent round leaves which come in whorls of three. In the variety *medio-variegatum* they are even more beautiful, each leaf having a yellow-cream blotch in the centre. Perhaps the plant is lovelier without its flowers. These come in dense clusters or heads at the end of the stems, and are pinkish in colour. They are at their best in late September, which makes this Sedum a valuable plant for the rockery – or for practically anywhere in the garden: a fine edging plant in the herbaceous-border, for instance. And a favourite window plant. A Japanese species, introduced as long ago as 1836, is named in honour of Philipp Franz von Siebold, who introduced many plants from Japan.

*S. spathulifolium* (*with spatula-shaped leaves*) also has leaves which

[1] Biennials are plants which bloom in the year following seed sowing, and then die. Common examples are Forgetmenot, Foxglove, Canterbury Bell, Sweet William. You will find that some of these sow themselves every year, seedlings springing up round the old plants.

many gardeners prefer to the flowers – in fact some gardeners cut them off as soon as they begin to show, though the varieties *purpureum* and *Capablanca* are more beautiful and are the two usually grown in our gardens. The first has thick, fleshy leaves in rosettes 2 inches wide; these are first mealy and white, then become a curiously beautiful plum-purple (glaucous and juicy-looking) and on starved soils are touched with bright crimson. The rosettes spread out and make thick fleshy mats of foliage for sheeting a wall or covering a flat boulder in the rockery. The variety *Capablanca* has white farinose (powdered) leaves and both plants are decorative enough for growing in pots indoors. Reverting to the subject of the flowers: they are golden yellow and come in clusters or heads at the end of hanging 4 inch stems; they are not particularly attractive and hanging over a wall look rather untidy.

*Sedum Sieboldii*

Finally, there are two well-known hybrid Sedums, one suitable for the border: Autumn Joy, sometimes known by its German name, *Herbstfreude,* a perennial 2 feet tall, with large flower-heads, salmon-pink tinged bronze (the parents are said to be *S. telphium* and *S. spectabile*); the other is Ruby Glow, which may be grown in the front row of the border or in the rockery – the usual place for it. It has flat heads of deep ruby-red flowers carried on lax stems about 9 inches tall (its parents are the trailing *S. cauticola* and Autumn Joy).

The last group of hardy succulents are the Sempervivums which are seldom grown indoors. One or two, however, *are* grown in pots because their foliage is so ornamental and interesting and are certainly worth a place on a window-sill in a living room. There are about 25 species, most of them from the mountainous regions of Central and Southern Europe: one is from Morocco. The generic name is derived from *semper vivo,* to live for ever. The so-called tender Houseleeks are now described under several different genera; some of the most desirable are the *Aeonium,* included in the next chapter.

The Common Houseleek is *Sempervivum tectorum* (*of the roofs of houses*) – another name is St. Patrick's Cabbage, but it is not so well known. This plant has been naturalised in Britain and is found on the roofs of houses and on walls in many districts but is not indigenous. It is the species most frequently seen in cultivation. It is a native of the mountains of Europe and is a tough, hardy plant surviving the snows and cold of high altitudes. On the lower slopes it usually grows in the crevices of rocks, where it makes mats of spreading rosettes, each rosette measuring 2 or 3 inches across; in some varieties they are much larger.

The rosettes of Sempervivums die after flowering, but numerous young plants or offsets are produced every year round the old ones and these perpetuate the original stock. The rooted pieces when detached quickly establish themselves and make new plants. It is possible to raise Houseleeks from seed, but as most of the species hybridise readily the seed seldom produces plants true to type; nevertheless some interesting forms and varieties will occasionally be found among the seedlings.

The Common Houseleek has open flattish rosettes with green succulent leaves tipped purple, the largest being about 2 inches long and $\frac{1}{2}$-inch wide. The flowers, purple-red, are borne at the end of hairy stems 8 to 12 inches tall and bloom, like those of the other kinds, during the summer months. There are several varieties, including Var. *calcareum,* from the French Alps, which has rosettes of glaucous leaves, tipped with brown, and smaller flowers; Var. *Monstrosum,* a variety with narrow, very succulent leaves; Var. *robustum,* a form larger in all its parts; and Var. *triste* (*dull*) with red-brown (perhaps *dull* brown) leaves and pink flowers.

The Cobweb Houseleek (*S. arachnoideum*), probably as well known as *S. tectorum,* has been called the most beautiful of all. It is just as easy to grow. And it is greatly admired for the cobweb effect of the whitish silken hairs that stretch from tip to tip of the pointed leaves (the specific epithet means covered with entangled hairs, giving the appearance of a spider's web). The leaves, reddish or green, form small rosettes about one to two inches across; and the flower-heads arise from the centres on stems 3 inches tall and are a charming shade of cherry-red. A singularly beautiful plant either in flower or without its flowers. This species has given numerous hybrids, both in the wild and in gardens. *S. x Funckii* is one of these – a complex hybrid, with both *S. tectorum* and the Cobweb Houseleek in its ancestory. The rosettes are compact, flattish, about $1\frac{1}{2}$ inches across, bright green in colour and covered with soft, glandular hair; the flowers, red-purple, have short petals and a dark eye.

*S. soboliferum* (*having creeping rooting stems*) is the popular Hen and Chickens Houseleek, a native of Northern Europe and Asia. It is so-named because it produces numerous offsets even among the leaves; these tiny offsets become quickly and easily detached and eventually root in the surrounding soil. The main rosettes are flattish, half-closed and about an inch wide, the leaves being smooth and pale green. The flowers, not often seen in cultivation, are greenish-yellow and borne on stems 4 to 8 inches tall. This attractive Sempervivum was planted by the great naturalist and botanist Linnaeus[1] in his garden in Sweden and offsets taken from the original plant as souvenirs by visitors are still growing and flourishing.

*S. x Thompsonii* is a hybrid between *S. arachnoideum* and *S. tectorum*; it has smaller rosettes than *S. tectorum*; its leaves are rather hairy and have tufts of white hairs at the tip; the flowers are the same size as those of the Cobweb Houseleek but the colour is not so vivid.

*S. Wulfenii* (probably commemorates Franz Xavier, Freiherr von Wulfen – 1728–1805 – Austrian botanical author). It resembles the Common Houseleek but has fewer leaves to its rosettes, which are about $3\frac{1}{2}$ inches across. The leaves are an attractive shade of grey-green and coloured purple at the base; and the flowers, greenish-yellow, are carried on hairy stems about 8 inches tall. Its offsets are usually few. The plant is a native of the Swiss and Austrian Alps.

All Sempervivums are easy to grow and increase. Most of them prosper in any light sandy loam; but the soil recommended by collectors consists of a light garden loam mixed with an equal part of brick-rubble powdered fine. Those that are grown in the crevices of a rock should be set in a handful of equal parts of sifted leafmould and fine sand; this richer medium will encourage strong and rapid root growth in places where space is naturally limited.

Many collectors of succulents plan a special border in their gardens for their plants. And, as I have already mentioned, most succulents (including cacti) benefit enormously from longish spells in the open. I have seen several of these borders in various districts and they are of course very different from our ordinary flower borders; they have an

[1] Carl Linnaeus, ennobled as Carl von Linné (1707–1778); he founded the system of the classification of plants which bears his name.

exotic look about them and bring a touch of the tropics to the garden. Is it advisable, by the way, to introduce some of the usual herbaceous plants in a succulents-border? Plants like Lupins and Delphiniums, for instance? I should say No to these two, certainly. But I think some of the silver-grey or white or glaucous foliage-plants accord well with any of the succulents one would use. There are many gardeners who condemn these borders as too artificial-looking and most of the landscape gardeners I know speak dispraisingly of them. However, I like to see them and I think if they are well planned they can be an important and attractive feature of any garden.

Ideally, a succulents border should be made up on a slight slope south or south-west so that it catches all the sun possible; on a slope the soil will be well drained and the plants seen to best advantage. The soil itself must be light and sandy; heavy loams and clay are quite useless for this type of border.

As the modern garden is on the small side, the border will very probably be limited in size – perhaps one 20ft. long by about 5ft. wide will be the most suitable. It is an excellent idea to sketch out the proposed border on paper, marking in the position and the approximate extent or size of the plants to be used (the latter point is important when a group or a clump of the same succulent is wanted – a good-sized clump of *Sedum spectabile,* for instance, could occupy a couple of square yards or more). In most of the borders I have seen in gardens pieces of good quality rockery stone are sunk into the soil at different intervals, some in the front row (several quite large pieces); others farther back and used as sort of background boulders to show up certain rare plants more conspicuously and at the same time protect them from strong winds. No soil is visible anywhere: all spaces between the plants are covered with pebbles, flints and sand, which give the final desert-like touch.

Beginning the arrangement of the plants with the edging or front row: use any of the hardy creeping kinds here. Widish mats of *Sedum spathulifolium purpureum* are beautiful and will soon spread and cover the edge of the pathway. Other suitable Sedums are the white fleshy-leaved variety Capablanca, and the more tender species *Sedum Sieboldii* (these plants were described in the preceding pages). The Houseleeks are also very suitable, forming flattish mats of fleshy rosettes which contrast well with the more colourful foliage of the Sedums. But a long row of mat-like plants, all about the same height, tends to monotony; consequently it is necessary to introduce here and there taller, contrasting things, such as some of the globose or cylindrical cacti, which in most districts would have to be sunk into the soil in their pots. They can be quite small, not more than about 9 inches tall or wide –

I am thinking especially of the flat-stemmed Opuntias, which would contrast perfectly with any of the mat-like succulents. Another cactus recommended for front-row planting is the popular Christmas or Crab Cactus (*Zygocactus truncatus*), either the ordinary plant (raised from cuttings, with its low drooping stems), or the taller, grafted kind; perhaps the former is better for the front-row position. The pot, or pots, should be sunk fairly near to the pathway. And gardeners who grow it in this position usually sink a smallish boulder behind it to prevent an excess of moisture reaching it, though in a well-drained pot it should be safe. Half-a-dozen plants arranged in a circle would give a really fine effect. (As I have already mentioned, this particular cactus needs as much fresh air as you can give it and to be left out in the open till quite late in the year – I have known it survive a slight frost or two.) Farther back – perhaps in the middle row – the grafted plant, grown to standard shape with a central stem, is a good choice and several planted together make an imposing group. In a small, narrow border a single specimen (sunk in its pot) is enough; in a wider border three planted crow's-foot fashion are recommended. Cover the rims of the pots entirely with small pebbles and let the pebbles extend to the plants in front. The Cobweb Houseleeks would be a perfect choice here, a drift of them reaching down to the pathway. Another suggestion is the Hottentot Fig (*Mesembryanthemum edulis*), whose fleshy trailing stems and leaves turn deep red in autumn. Clumps of this attractive succulent look well on each side of the Christmas Cactus and may also be planted behind it (or a clump of it) at the top of the border.

The back row plants will be the tallest. There are unfortunately only a few really hardy succulents suitable for this position: both *Sedum spectabile* and *S. telephium* (and their varieties) are about the tallest; but these may be considered too close to the showy herbaceous perennials I have already condemned. Perhaps these Sedums are best used to fill up an empty space at the end, or at each end of a border. I have seen them used in this way and overshadowed – overwhelmed almost – by some of the majestic Agaves. These are excellent for the back row but may be too large for the small border. If, however, you have room for them, set three in a row. I recommend *Agave Parryi* (page 125), which is among the smaller species and is reasonably hardy. Next to them grow some of the smaller Yuccas,[1] such as *Yucca flaccida* and *Y. glauca*. Yuccas have tough-looking, long, narrow, pointed leaves and tall spikes of (usually) creamy-white flowers in late summer (various species are described in the following chapter).

Some of the hardiest of the Opuntias may also be used as back row plants; three or four could be set between the Agaves and the Yuccas,

[1] Yuccas are usually included in books on Succulents, but botanically they are known as Xerophytes (i.e. plants that can live in places where water is scarce).

though as most of them will be pot-grown and consequently housed in winter they won't be very tall. They are more commonly grown as middle-row plants. The charming low-growing *Opuntia microdasys,* with its flat green pads studded with tufts of golden-yellow glochids, is one of the best. Grow this choice cactus in groups, if you can, and cover the rims of the pots with sand and pebbles. The pebbles and sand may, if you wish, extend backward to the Agaves and Yuccas, or good-sized pieces of rock may be set in the soil behind the cacti. Rocks and boulders make a perfect background for any cacti and succulent plants we want to grow in a border.

Many are stiff, rigid-looking things and need, I think, some of the soft, flowing foliage-plants I mentioned above: Artemisias, for instance (silver, grey, white) and that favourite bedder, the white velvety-leaved *Senecio cineraria.* This *Senecio* can be grown in a pot and sunk into the soil and lifted again when it is time to put out (in its place) the tender cacti and succulents. It is easily raised from seed and may be grown on in pots and planted out in the garden at practically any time of the year.

*Senecio cineraria,* by the way, is often grown in conjunction with Yuccas and when set among them and in front of them (as a sort of undergrowth) has a softening effect on the tall stiff-looking plants.

Another foliage-plant that may be similarly used is the dwarf Lavender Cotton, *Santolina chamaecyparissus var. nana.* Both the type, a taller plant, and the variety are best renewed (by cuttings) every year, as they grow straggly and flop untidily on the soil after a season or two.

This dwarf silver-grey foliage-plant (var. *nana*) is among the most useful and delightful of evergreens for formal edging, and may be kept down to a height of 6 inches by clipping it carefully in July, just before the flower-buds open.

Of the Artemisias, *Artemisia frigida,* with finely divided silver-grey foliage and about 12 inches tall, is one of the choicest for growing in a succulent border. It is especially useful as a foil-plant to some of the taller spiny Opuntias and the magnificent *Sansevieria* which have stiff, flat, sword-like leaves. (See chapter 6, page 184).

The best kind of border, whether it is to accommodate herbaceous plants or succulents, is the one planned against a wall or a strong wooden fence. A wall makes the most attractive of all backgrounds; furthermore, it is permanent and it provides a certain amount of warmth and shelter from winds and protection from frost. Hedges are not so good for herbaceous plants, especially those requiring plenty of moisture, as the hungry roots of most hedging plants quickly impoverish the soil. On the other hand, certain kinds, such as Yew or

Box, clipped back neat and square and kept reasonably low, would be all right for plants sunk in their pots into the soil.

Then there are those borders which have no background; these are planned on the flat, with a gravel pathway running along the front, and grass, usually a lawn, behind. One can walk round them and view the plants from all sides. Planned in this way, they are really beds, not borders; a border implies a background of some sort. In several gardens I have seen borders cut out in the middle of a lawn – average size of border (or bed): 20 feet by 6 feet. Most of them were filled with tender succulents planted out in their pots. A lawn is not the best setting for cacti and succulents. They look incongruous in grass – cacti especially, which one associates with sand and dry arid places. The grass looks much less conspicuous, however, when these beds are edged with some low evergreen such as Box, clipped topiary-fashion, square and solid, about 9 inches wide and high.

# Chapter Six
# Tender Succulents

Plant-lovers living in towns and cities, without a garden, can give their plants an airing only in window-boxes, provided, of course, there are ledges big enough to support the boxes. If there are not, then the plants must be stood on a sill indoors and the window left open when the weather is suitable. Indoor gardeners need not despair, then: all they have to remember is to choose the smallest plants or those that in the course of years grow very slowly. The vast majority of cacti and tender succulents do. And they don't take up much room. The average-sized window-sill can accommodate at least a dozen pots.

Florists usually have a good display of these plants and are able to give prospective customers plenty of hints on growing them.

People with more time to spare will no doubt go farther afield – perhaps by car at week-ends – and visit specialist nurseries and botanic gardens and see cacti and succulents being tended by skilled professional gardeners. This is the best way to study the plants; it is the way most botanists get their information; only the priviledged few can travel thousands of miles to see the plants growing in their natural habitats.

The world-famous Kew Gardens, near London, has a remarkably fine collection of cacti in the wonderful Sherman Hoyt Cactus House. Adjoining Houses contain tender succulents such as the extraordinary *Lithops*, which imitate the stones among which they grow (an astonishing example of mimicry in plants); and *Cheiridopsis, Conophytum, Faucaria, Pleiospilos*, are others, which like the *Lithops* are all small enough for the indoor gardener to grow in pots and pans or indeed in a single container stood on a window-sill. *Conophytum* are especially recommended to those townspeople who want to grow some attractive and interesting succulents in small containers: they will find that they can probably get 50 or more different species or varieties in a pan about 12 inches square.

Most of the tender succulents described in the following pages are obtainable from specialist nurseries; I have, however, included some which are a little difficult to get at present. It is worth while to try and get seeds of these, though, from seed specialists.

*Adromischus Cooperi* is one of the popular tender succulents. It is a small plant, like the other species, and therefore very suitable for indoor gardeners who have only a limited amount of space for their cacti and succulents. Only 3 or 4 different species, of about 20, are offered by nurseries; and *A. Cooperi* seems to be the favourite – it is often labelled *A. festivus*. Like all the *Adromischus*, it is a native of South-west Africa. Its fleshy rounded leaves, an inch long and $\frac{3}{4}$-inch wide, come on very short stems and are grey-green flecked with red-brown on both sides. The flowers are $\frac{1}{2}$-inch long and pinkish. This species was named in honour of Thomas Cooper (1815–1913), an English gardener and botanist, who collected many well-known plants in South Africa.

A species, often on show in florists' windows, is *A. maculatus* (spotted), with delightful, spotted or blotched, fat, fleshy leaves, and in my opinion, a more attractive plant than *A. Cooperi*. The leaves are kidney-shaped, flattish above and very convex below (they look full of juice), grey-green in colour and beautifully marked with purplish-brown. They come on very short stems, not visible from above, and lie huddled together on the stones where the plants grow. The flowers, as in all the species, are by no means showy; they come in a long raceme (or cluster) and are deep pink with pale pink tips. (The word *Adromischus* is from *adros*, strong; and *miskos*, a flower-stem; it refers to the stout-looking flower-stem).

As *Adromischus* were formerly included in the genus *Cotyledon* they are sometimes found labelled with this name. So you may sometimes be offered *Cotyledon Cooperi* and *C. maculatus*.

The cultivation of the plants is the same as for Cotyledon. They need a sunny position and a temperature which must not fall below 45F (7C) or 50F (10C) in winter. From November to about April they need very little water. Grow them in a compost consisting of light loamy soil mixed with plenty of finely-powdered mortar rubble. Keep the soil moist during the growing season. Both plants, like all *Adromischus*, are slow growers and seldom produce strong enough side shoots which could be used for cuttings. The best way to propagate *Adromischus* is by leaf-cuttings.

The genus belongs to the *Family Crassulaceae*, which contains many small succulent plants very suitable for growing in pots indoors.

*Aeonium* is a genus which also belongs to the *Crassula Family* and the species described here and offered by nurseries are cultivated like *Adromischus*. All these plants appreciate an airing in the hot sunshine and, when possible, should be sunk in the ground in their pots. Many of the Aeoniums eventually make tall plants and are consequently

more at home in a greenhouse border than in a pot. But it is possible
to obtain new young plants quite frequently by propagation: one
simply cuts off the top of the plant (a portion of the stem with the head
or rosette), and uses it as a cutting. Leave these cut stems for 24 hours
to enable the sap to dry and then insert them in well-moistened silver
sand; cover with a bell-glass (or use a propagating case) and leave
in a shady greenhouse till roots have formed. Two of our species,
*Aeoium arboreum* and *A. Haworthii*, grow tall, their branches measuring
about 2 or 3 feet in length; the other two are small and may be left for
years undisturbed in their pots.

*Aeonium arboreum*

*Aeonium* are related to *Sempervivum* and some of the species are
still described under that name. There are about 40 species and they
are found in the Mediterranean region and parts of North Africa, in
the Canary Islands, Madeira and other Atlantic Islands. *Aeonium* is the

name used by Dioscoridęs (a Greek physician of the 1st century) for the species *A. arboreum*.

*A. arboreum* (*growing in tree-like form*) is a native of Morocco and widely distributed in the Mediterranean region. The plant offered by most nurseries and florists, however, is the variety *A. arboreum atropurpureum*, which has dense rosettes of dark purple leaves and racemes, about 9 inches long, of winter-blooming, golden-yellow flowers. When fully grown it reaches a height of about 3 feet; the rosettes are always attractive, with the individual leaves measuring about 2 inches long and $\frac{1}{2}$-inch wide. This variety and another called Zwarkop (with even richer coloured leaves) are less fastidious in cultivation than the type, which needs protection from bright summer sunshine. The sap of this plant is used by fishermen in Portugal to harden lines.

*A. Goochiae* is found in the Canary Islands and is one of the smaller convenient-sized species for a pot or a pan. It makes a shrubby plant with spreading stems about 6 inches high and has flattish rosettes of rather sticky leaves, olive-green in colour. The flowers come in clusters about 2 inches across; they are a pretty shade of pink and usually at their best in early summer. It is often grown in a hanging-basket, for the stems have a tendency to trail as they grow and mature.

*A. Haworthii*, also from the Canary Islands, is one of the tall-growing species, its branches finally reaching a height of about two feet; but in its young state it makes a desirable little pot-plant, with very attractive bluish-green rosettes, the individual leaves being edged with a red-brown horny substance. The flowers are usually pale yellow tinged with pink (sometimes they are creamy-white) and bloom in April and May. The species is named in honour of Adrian Hardy Haworth (1768–1833), who was a specialist on succulent plants and published in 1794 a monograph on the genus *Mesembryanthemum*. This *Aeonium* is one of the more popular kinds grown by collectors; it benefits from being stood outside in the open air during the summer months; if it is kept permanently indoors it should be protected from the hot summer sun.

*A. Simsii* is another Canary Island species and a small, neat plant which is ideal for growing in a pot. It is described as one of the more hardy kinds but most collectors keep it permanently indoors. It is a densely tufted plant very much like a *Sempervivum* and produces many offsets. The rosettes measure from one to three inches across and consist of usually erect strap-shaped leaves, the biggest being two inches long and $\frac{1}{4}$-inch wide. They are edged with short hairs; from the centre of the rosettes arise 4-inch stems carrying flattish clusters of tiny golden-yellow flowers. I have often seen this species labelled

*Sempervivum Simsii* and it is occasionally offered in shops under that name. Crossed with *Aeonium canariense*, a species with enormous rosettes (3 feet across), and also with *A. spathulatum*, it has produced some very attractive hybrids. *A. Simsii* is named in honour of John Sims (1749–1831), a physician and botanist, who edited *Curtis's Botanical Magazine* from 1800 to 1826. Some species are difficult to come by nowadays: *A. lindleyi* is one of these; I have seen it in a few collections. It is a native of Palma and Tenerife and is prized for its lovely long-lasting golden-yellow flowers. It resembles *A. Goochiae* (described above) in its sticky leaves, but is a taller bigger plant than that species.

*Aloe ausana*

Aloes are favourite indoor plants and most catalogues list about a dozen different species; only one (*A. aristata*), described in the preceding chapter, is hardy enough for growing in the open. See page 126. The best known is the Partridge-breasted *Aloe* (*A. variegata; irregularly coloured*; referring to the dark green leaves striped with white; see page 127). It is usually stemless and produces plenty of offsets. (These root easily in warm, sandy soil and should be used to increase one's stock.) The leaves, 5 inches long, are triangular, erect and beautifully marked with bands of white blotches. The flowers are red and come in a loose spike about 12 inches in length. I should say it was the most popular of all the succulent plants grown indoors. It dislikes too much bright sunshine, and for this reason usually does better in an ordinary living-room than in a greenhouse. Do not let water collect at the base of the leaves, as it will cause rotting and the plant may perish. A closely-related species (difficult to get however) is *Aloe ausana*; it is very similar to *A. variegata* and may well be a variety of that plant. Both are natives of Cape Province.

*A. africana* (African) is one of the species that produces long stems (see page 126). It is a native of Cape Province and has a stem about 12 feet tall; the leaves are usually recurved, glaucous green, $2\frac{1}{2}$ inches wide and about 18 inches long, with large teeth along the edges. The flowers, borne in dense racemes, are deep yellow, but never produced in cultivation. This Aloe grows slowly indoors, and is best repotted, like the others, every third year. Trimming the roots, which is necessary, keeps these pot-grown Aloes conveniently small.

*A. arborescens* (*tending to be woody; or tree-like*) is another tall-growing Aloe in nature but seldom gets very big in a pot indoors and it may be kept quite dwarf by repotting and pruning the roots. It produces suckers at the base of the stem; the leaves, pale green and glaucous, are 12 inches long, narrow and toothed; they form attractive rosettes, from which arise the close spikes of red flowers. This species is a native of Natal, Zululand, Transvaal, Southern Rhodesia.

*A. brevifolia* (*with short leaves*) is one of the naturally-small species and has branching stems, with rosettes 4 inches wide consisting of very thick, pale green, glaucous leaves, toothed along the margins. The flowers are red (but seldom seen in cultivation) and are borne in close spikes on short stems. This species makes an attractive foliage plant for a pot or pan.

*Aloe ferox*

149

*A. ferox* (*very thorny*) is a tall, spiny plant from Cape Province and Natal, its stems often reaching 10 feet or more in height. Its leaves have reddish spines along the margins and also on the upper and lower surfaces; they are long and tapering and form attractive dense rosettes. The flowers are carried in conical spikes and are deep orange in colour. This is said to be the spiniest of all the Aloes we grow. In winter its glaucous-blue foliage is always much admired.

*A. Greenii* is a stemless species from Natal and a favourite plant for a smallish pot or pan. It is another Aloe with attractive foliage. Its leaves, about 15 inches long, are bright green and marked with bands of whitish-green on both surfaces. Its flowers when they appear come in loose spikes and are dull red.

*A. humilis* (*low-growing: smaller than most of its kindred*); this *Aloe*, from Cape Province, is most collectors' choice after the Partridge-breasted *Aloe* (*A. variegata*). It remains a small neat plant after many years and seldom needs repotting. It is stemless and produces dense rosettes of glaucous green leaves (4 inches long and ½-inch wide); these are very thick and fleshy and have close, large spiny teeth along the edges. The flowers come in long racemes and are yellow or red. There are many varietal forms.

Some more stemless or almost stemless kinds are *A. Pienaari*; this plant has dark green, narrow, erect leaves, which are toothed along the edges; the flowers are scarlet in the bud and open to lemon-yellow. *A. Pienaari* grows slowly and, unlike *A. humilis*, does not make any offsets. It is a native of Southern Rhodesia and North Transvaal. *A. polyphylla* (*with many leaves*) has rosettes consisting of 60 or more spirally-arranged pale green leaves, which are toothed and have lighter green margins. No-one yet has come across a specimen which has flowered. It is a native of Basutoland. *A. striata* (*striped*) is usually stemless and has dense rosettes of pale glaucous grey leaves about 18 inches long with pinkish-white stripes along the margins; the edges are quite smooth. The flowers are pendulous and an attractive shade of coral-red; the plant has produced some desirable hybrid forms.

The cultivation of Aloes in pots is quite simple: they need a winter temperature of round about 45F (7C) and protection from draughts; they usually prosper well when grown in a fairly subdued light – they should never be exposed for long periods to hot sunshine. Water them regularly during the growing season and keep them reasonably dry when they are resting. Propagation is mostly by offsets – it is certainly the easiest method, for roots have usually formed while these offsets are attached to the mother plant.

*Ceropegia* come from South Africa and other tropical and sub-tropical countries. The only species listed in catalogues seems to be *C. Stapelii-*

*formis,* a native of Cape Province. There are roughly 100 different species and occasionally one comes across a few of the most attractive kinds in a cool greenhouse or a conservatory. *Ceropegia* are trailing or twining plants well adapted to hanging-baskets or for training up the stems of plant like Tree Ferns. The flowers of many of the species resemble those of the *Stapelia* (see page 192). *C. stapeliiformis* has thick fleshy stems, grey-green with purplish markings; the leaves are reduced to scales as in *Stapelia*; the flowers are more curious than beautiful; they are over two inches long, slender and tubular in shape and marked with purple on the swollen base. This plant may be trained up wires or a slender bamboo cane and kept to a reasonable height by topping it every now and then. *C. Sandersonii* and *C. Woodii* I have seen growing in hanging-baskets; they make charming trailing plants but unfortunately are rarely offered by any of the nurseries nowadays. Both species are natives of Natal. *C. Sandersonii* is a quick-growing species, with purplish succulent stems; and heart-shaped succulent leaves. The flowers are large, nearly 3 inches long, pale green marked with dark green spots and curiously-shaped: the corolla tube is narrow and at the top the lobes are expanded to form a wide canopy-like structure. *C. Woodii* has a large corm, which must be planted with the top well above the soil. It produces slender trailing stems (often 3 feet long), carrying small succulent leaves beautifully variegated with white and purple; the flowers, pitcher-shaped, and quite small, are purple. Both plants bloom in early summer.

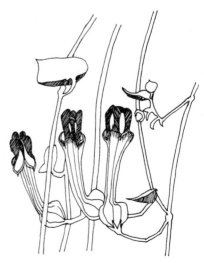

*Ceropegia Woodii*

151

Grow *Ceropegia* in a compost of equal parts of light garden loam, sifted leafmould and coarse washed sand; the temperature of the room (or greenhouse) must not fall below 45F (7C) in winter, when, by the way, it is necessary to water only to keep the soil from becoming desert-dry. The plants need spraying and watering regularly all through the summer months. Propagation is mostly by cuttings: take small side shoots in spring and insert them in pots of sand and stand in a propagating case.

*Ceropegia* belong to the *Family Asclepiadaceae*; and the generic name is from *Keros,* wax; and *pege*, a fountain; many of the flowers have a wax-like appearance.

*Cheiridopsis peculiaris*

*Cheiridopsis* are small succulent plants from South Africa (from Great and Little Namaqualand) and need full sunlight and complete protection from frost. Only two species are currently listed in nurserymen's catalogues. Both were at one time included in the genus *Mesembryanthemum* and may sometimes still be found labelled with that generic name and described as 'tender', 'difficult' *Mesembryanthemums*. The chief thing to remember is to keep these plants in a warm well-ventilated room during the winter months. *Cheiridopsis* are among the most curious of all the succulents we grow indoors. The name is from the Greek *cheiris*, sleeve, and *opis*, like; referring to the sleeve-like form of the withered sheathing leaves. The name helps to describe the peculiar character of the leaves of some of the species: the leaf-sheaths, when dead and dried, remain to protect the new leaves during the resting season. *C. peculiaris* is usually singled out as the species with the most interesting shape. One pair of leaves (each leaf is 1½ inches long and an inch wide) is united at the base only; these leaves spread out wide and lie flat on the soil. Above them grow up a pair of united leaves, through, which the next pair grows, the united pair remaining, when dead, as sheaths to protect the new leaves. During the summer months it is essential to keep the plants dry to enable the sheaths to develop fully. The growing and feeding season is the autumn. The flowers of *C. peculiaris* are yellow, daisy-like, about $1\frac{1}{2}$ inches across and come on shortish stems. Unfortunately this uncommonly beautiful little succulent is rarely listed in nurseryman's catalogue nowadays. The two offered are *C. candidissima* (synonym: *Mesembryanthemum candidissimum*) and *C. cigarettifera* (*M. cigarettiferum*). Both are stem-less and form clumps. The first has thick, fleshy leaves, 3 inches long and $\frac{1}{2}$-inch wide, whitish in colour with dark green dots; the flowers, an inch across, are white or pinkish. The specific epithet means very white and refers to the general appearance of the plant. It is one of the Mimicry plants and often difficult to find among the stones and pebbles in the wild. *C. cigarettifera* has slender succulent leaves about an inch long, grey-green in colour; the specific epithet refers to the cigarette-like appearance of the long white sheaths which protect the young slender leaves. The flowers are an attractive shade of golden-yellow. *Cheiridopsis* need a well-drained compost consisting of equal parts of loam, sifted leafmould and crushed mortar rubble (or equal quantities of rubble and silver sand). Propagation is usually from seeds or by cutting – both, of course, require gentle heat in a greenhouse.

*Conophytum*, like *Cheiridopsis* and several other genera were once included in *Mesembryanthemum*. (See page 177 and also *Faucaria*; *Lithops*; *Pleiospilos*.) Although there are about 260 different species (natives of Namaqualand, South Africa) only a few are in general cultivation. The generic name is from *konos*, cone; and *phyton*, plant; and refers to the shape of the plants. They have thick succulent leaves or plant-bodies and, like *Cheiridopsis*, are difficult to find among the stones and pebbles of the desert regions where they grow. They are small (some not more than $\frac{1}{2}$-inch tall) and thus very useful for massing in pans and other similar containers (see page 144). These fascinating Mimicry plants are divided into two groups, viz. the lobed kinds (2-lobate); and those whose fat succulent leaves have flat or convex tops.

*C. albescens*; *C. bilobum*; *C. Elishae* are examples of the first group; they usually begin to grow in May and they flower in summer, nearly a month before the other kind though the growing and the resting periods often vary according to the district in which the plants are cultivated. *C. albescens* (*whitish*; referring to the whitish-grey colouring of the plant-body – or thick fat leaves); this *Conophytum* grows about an inch tall; the leaves are 2-lobed; the slits or clefts (forming the lobes) are distinct, being about ¼-inch deep. The flowers are yellow and about an inch across. They arise from the clefts or slits and are roughly star- or daisy-shaped. *C. bilobum* (2-lobed) has fat, pale-green leaves, the lobes having blunt tips; the flowers, an inch across, are deep yellow. *C. Elishae* forms clumps and flowers freely, the flowers being ½-inch across and yellow; the plant-body (2-lobed) is greyish-green and marked with purple.

Of the broad, flat-topped species, *Conophytum Pearsonii* is one of the best known. The plant-body, about ¾-inch high and almost the same in width, closely resembles the fat succulent growths of the Pebble Plants – *Lithops. C. Pearsonii* eventually forms dense clumps; and the older growths are usually much smaller than the young. They are an attractive shade of blue-green; the flat tops each have a tiny fissure from which grow the inch-wide, rose-mauve flowers. During the resting period (usually May and June) the plant bodies shrivel and form a protective parchment-like skin to the new leaves, which develop within them. During this time no watering is necessary – the plants are kept completely dry. Mist-spraying may commence when the flower-buds appear in the summer. *Conophytums* growing and flowering in a greenhouse appreciate some shade during hot bright summer weather. The compost used for *Cheiridopsis*, with a little extra leafmould, is ideal for them.

*Cotyledon simplicifolia* is a hardy alpine plant now called *Chiastophyllum oppositifolium* and was described in the preceding chapter (page 129). Many of the other species are also separated into different genera; so we have *Echeveria nuda* which was formerly *Cotyledon nuda*; *Pachyphytum bracteosum* (*C. Pachyphytum,* now a synonym); *Umbilicus pendulinus* (syn. *C. Umbilious*); and there are many others that have been renamed. *Cotyledon,* according to present-day botanists, consists of about 30 species and are all tender plants which must be grown in a cool greenhouse or in a room where the temperature remains round about 45F (7C). The two most popular species are *C. orbiculata* and *C. undulata.* Various other kinds are offered from time to time by nurseries; both *C. jacobensiana* and the tiny *C. ladysmithiensis* are charming small plants and much valued for indoor decoration. *C. orbiculata* (*round and flat*) is, like most of the species, a native of South Africa. It has thick round leaves, with a small tip, and narrow at the base; their great attraction is their soft grey waxy covering. The flowers, which bloom in summer, come in small hanging clusters, and are yellowish-red. This is a charming little succulent, even without its flowers, and deserves a place in every collection. It is a variable species and has produced several desirable varieties; the loveliest is *C.*

*orbiculata var. oophylla* (*oo,* egg; *phylla,* leaf), which has very small egg-shaped leaves, densely frosted or powdered white. Neither this plant nor the following should be watered overhead if the white substance on the leaves is to be preserved. *C. undulata* (*waved*) is singled out by gardeners as the most attractive of all the species. It has leaves about 4 inches long, narrowed at the base, broad at the top, the edge being beautifully waved. They are thickly covered with meal and always much admired. The flowers, $\frac{3}{4}$-inch long, are cream with a red stripe. These Cotyledons are shrubby plants and easily propagated by seeds, cuttings and leaf cuttings. The ideal compost for these succulents consists of garden loam mixed with plenty of coarse sand and crushed mortar rubble. They need dry conditions through the winter months. The name *Cotyledon* is from the Greek *kotyle*, a cavity or cup, referring to the cup-like leaves of *Cotyledon Umbilicus*, which plant is now (as mentioned above) *Umbilicus pendulinus. Cotyledon* belong to the Crassula Family, *Crassulaceae.*

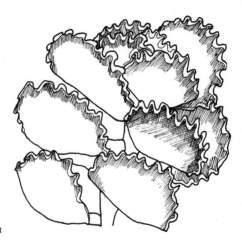

*Cotyledon undulata*

*Crassula* is a large genus; there are about 300 different species, most of them occurring in South Africa. Only one is hardy (*Crassula sarcocaulis* – already described; see page 129); the tender kinds offered by nurseries and florists make excellent pot-plants for warm sunny rooms. In summer give them plenty of water; in winter – from about November onward – keep them reasonably dry. There are, however, a few Mimicry species which must be watched over; keep them in a room where the winter temperature doesn't drop below 50F (10C) and remember they have a resting period in summer. The easier *Crassula* need the same sort of treatment as *Cotyledon* (see above), the same sort of soil, and are increased by seeds, cuttings or leaf-cuttings.

*Crassula arborescens* (*tree-like*) is a native of Cape Province, where it grows to bush size. It is a shrubby type and reaches a height of 2 or 3 feet in a sunny greenhouse: in its habitat it is said to form a large 12foot bush. Grown in a pot, however, it remains small and neat for many years. Its leaves are roundish, fleshy, grey-green with red margins and dotted red on the upper surface. The flowers come in terminal clusters and are white at first, then turn red, but they seldom appear on cultivated plants. Some gardeners have succeeded in getting this plant to bloom by growing it in a fairly dry soil and keeping it in a cool, sunny greenhouse.

*C. arta* is a native of Namaqualand and is one of the smallest species; it forms clumps of very short branching stems bearing tiny, closely-packed pale green mealy leaves with raised grey lines. The flowers are white and come in small clusters. This is one of the Mimicry Crassula and should be kept fairly dry during its resting period (this resting period, as I have already mentioned, varies with the district – say, cold north or warm south – where the plants are grown). It likes winter sunshine and complete protection from draughts.

*Crassula arta*

*C. barbata* (*with long weak hairs*), a native of South Africa, is another Mimicry species. It forms stemless rosettes 1½ inches across of broad, green leaves, which are curved inward, and have long, white hairs along the edge. The flowers are white and come in small close heads. After the flowers have faded the rosette dies; but offsets are usually formed round the parent plant and these continue to grow and will produce flowers the following season.

*C. cordata* (*heart-shaped*) comes from South-East Africa and has slender stems, with heart-shaped, fleshy leaves, $\frac{3}{4}$-inch long, covered with white meal, and are red at the margin. This Crassula is a most attractive plant for a pot and may eventually reach a height of 12 inches. The flowers are white and appear in summer, and among them adventitious (accidental) buds are often produced – normally, of course, the flower-buds appear first.

*C. corymbulosa* (*with flowers produced in a corymb*[1]), a native of Cape Province, produces rosettes of narrow leaves crowded on very short stems; the rosettes at the time of flowering become more slender and longer and die when the flowers have faded. But new offsets always appear round the old plant and grow on into strong new plants during the following spring. The flowers are white and come in long open clusters.

*C. deceptrix* (*deceptive*; probably refers to the mimicry character of the plant); a species from Namaqualand and one of the Mimicry species, with a summer resting period. Its very short, branching stems form clumps of fat fleshy leaves; these are about $\frac{3}{4}$-inch long, flat above and almost hemispherical (half-spherical) beneath; they are whitish-grey in colour and covered with raised lines. The flowers are white and carried in slender clusters. This *Crassula* needs a warm well-ventilated room during the cold winter months.

*C. deltoides* (*triangular*; referring to the shape of the leaves), another species from Namaqualand and a good choice for growing in a pot in an ordinary living-room. Its great attraction is its fat fleshy leaves, grey-green and mealy, with the upper surfaces grooved, and the lower bluntly keeled (roughly speaking, boat-shaped); like most of the Crassulas we grow indoors, *C. deltoides* produces small insignificant flowers – they are dirty white and quite uninteresting.

*C. falcata* (*sickle-shaped*) may sometimes be found in florists' show-windows labelled *Rochea falcata*, which is now a synonym. This is one of the few species that bears attractive flowers; these are scarlet and are borne in close flat showy clusters at the end of the stems, which may be 2 or 3 feet tall. The leaves are thick and fleshy, sickle-shaped, very conspicuous, almost horizontal on the fleshy stems, and grey-green in colour. This species makes a charming pot-plant for a room and is one of the easiest to grow. It blooms in summer and when it reaches a good height, say 12 inches or so, it is wise to support the stem with a thin wooden stake (perhaps a bamboo) inserted in the soil. *C. falcata* is propagated by stem cuttings, leaf cuttings and from seeds. The plant is a native of Cape Province.

[1] A corymb is a cluster of flowers in which the outer stalks are longer than the inner ones.

*C. Gilii,* from the province of Natal in South Africa, forms clumps of almost stemless rosettes, the leaves of which are glaucous green, ovalish and fringed with small hairs; these leaves lie closely one above another. The flowers are white and come in round clusters on long stems and are much less attractive than the leaves.

*C. Justi-Corderoyi* is a favourite plant with growers of Crassulas and is named in honour of Mr. Justas Corderoy who was a well-known English collector of succulents. Very little is known about its origin; it may well be a hybrid but it was not raised by the collector named above. It has short erect stems which branch from the base and are furnished with narrow, tapering, dark green leaves blotched with red. The flowers are pink and come in smallish clusters. It is another of the easy ones to grow and make a fine ornamental plant for a room.

*C. lactea (milk-coloured)* is recommended by growers for its sweetly-scented, milk-white flowers, small and star-shaped, which are carried in loose racemes at the end of the stems. 'A decorative, easy plant,' says a florist, 'and one I am always being asked for. It blooms in winter and thrives in a livingroom.' It is one of the shrubby species with longish (2-foot) stems, which are woody at the base. The leaves, ovalish, about 1½ inches long, are joined at the base and are smooth, dark green and have white dots along the margins. Many people who grow it put it outside during the summer to encourage strong vigorous growth of the stems. This species occurs in Natal and the Transvaal.

*C. lycopodioides* (resembling *Lycopodium* or Club-moss) is a species from South West Africa where it produces branching stems 12 inches tall completely hidden by tiny scale-like leaves (the Club-moss has similar scale-like leaves covering its stems). These leaves, an attractive deep green, are arranged like tiles, and produce a four-angled effect; the flowers are tiny and grow from the leaf axils (joints); they are yellow and quite inconspicuous. This is one of the easily grown Crassulas and prospers in any warm sunny living-room. There are several varieties of this plant in cultivation. Perhaps the best known is *C. lycopodioides var. monstrosa (abnormal)*, with more freely-branching stems and leaves not so regularly arranged, nor pressed so close against the stems. With its deep rich green colouring, I think it is a more beautiful plant than the other. It is smaller, too, and makes a good table decoration. Often the growth reverts to the normal type. It is also from S.W. Africa.

*C. multicava (many hollows;* referring to the leaves); a shrubby species found in various parts of South Africa. Its leaves are blue-green with a reddish tinge, roughly heart-shaped, with the surfaces finely but deeply pitted. The reddish tinge becomes more conspicuous in the summer when the plant is stood for long periods in the sun. The flowers appear in late spring and are a pretty shade of pink. This Crassula makes a handsome foliage plant for a sunny room; like the other easy-to-grow kinds, it needs plenty of water during the summer months.

*C. obliqua* (*lopsided, oblique;* referring to the posture or disposition of the leaves). This is another favourite shrubby type for growing in a living-room. It is a most attractive pot plant, with thick light green somewhat egg-shaped leaves; these are tapering, blunt-tipped and have scattered dots on the surfaces. This species was apparently widely cultivated by the Hottentots (natives inhabiting the Cape of Good Hope) who used the roots for food. *C. obliqua* is often confused with *C. portulacea,* which is described below.

*C. perfosa* (*pierced through:* referring to the appearance of the leaves, through which the stems seem to be threaded); a singularly beautiful plant (from Cape Province) for a hanging-basket or a largish pot. The fleshy leaves are ovalish, pointed and glaucous, with reddish dots, and are united in pairs all along the stems; these are decumbent (lying on the ground) and are about 12 inches long. The flowers are small, yellowish, and come in loose open clusters.

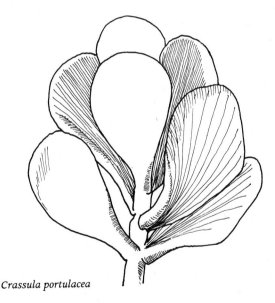

*Crassula portulacea*

*C. portulacea* is one of the toughest of all the Crassulas we grow as house plants. With its shining green ovalish leaves and long thick stem it resembles *C. obliqua,* (see above) except that in *C. portulacea*

159

the leaves are red at the margins. The flowers, which are white, come in terminal clusters and bloom in winter. But it has been found that they appear only if the plant is left to grow in its pot outdoors all through the summer months. In fact, it is best kept outside till the frosty weather sets in. The name used here is now a synonym and the correct specific name is *Crassula argentea*. The plant is a native of Cape Province.

*C. Schmidtii* is one of the few Crassulas with attractive flowers: they are a charming shade of deep carmine and contrast beautifully with the rosettes of slender tapering fleshy green leaves. It makes a delightful small pot plant for a room. This species is also from Cape Province.

*C. socialis* (*forming colonies*) makes fairly dense mats of tiny rosettes, about ½-inch across, the leaves forming them being triangular-shaped, light green in colour and somewhat toothed. It is an excellent plant for a pan and a good companion for *C. Cooperi,* another mat-forming species, with crowded pale green leaves about ½-inch long, and pale pink flowers. Both species are from Cape Province.

*C. tetragona* (*tetra,* 4; *gonia,* angle) is one of the shrubby species and has erect, branching fleshy stems up to about two feet tall. The thick juicy-looking leaves, which are joined at the base, are about an inch long, tapering, and curve upward at the end; they are almost cylindrical but slightly flat along the top surface, and round or squarish in cross-section. The flowers are white and come in small clusters. As already mentioned (page 130), Crassulas like the same sort of soil as Cotyledons.

*Echeveria* belong to the *Crassula Family*. The genus contains about 150 different species, all natives of America and very abundant in California, Mexico and Texas. They were formerly included in *Cotyledon,* but are quite distinct from those plants; the leaves, for instance, are always in rosettes. The name commemorates Athanasio Echeverriay Godoy, a botanical artist who did many of the drawings for *Flora Mexicana,* published at the beginning of the nineteenth century. Echeverias are cultivated like Cotyledons, and the chief method of propagating them is by dividing up the clumps of rosettes. Leaf cuttings may also be taken; they root very readily. Less often are seeds sown, since Echeverias hybridise very freely and as a rule produce a curious mixture of types. Hybridisation is usually left to the expert breeder; *E. x derosa,* between *E. derenbergii* and *E. setosa,* is a well-known plant and widely grown.

One species, at least (*Echeveria glauca*), will be familiar to most gardeners; it is the species used – and is still in use, I believe – in summer bedding; and it will often be seen in ribbon-planting, the method of setting plants out in lines or bands of colour to form attractive designs. *E. glauca* (formerly *E. secunda glauca*) occurs in Mexico and has compact rosettes, 4 inches across, the leaves being a delightful shade of blue-grey with red margins and rounded in shape ($\frac{3}{4}$-inch at the base), with a short tip. The flowers, on longish stems, are bell-shaped, light red and yellow at the mouth. These, by the way, are always removed in bedding-out schemes, as they would obviously spoil the flat carpet effect of the design.

*E. derenbergii* is from Mexico, occurring chiefly in the State of Oaxaca, facing the Pacific. The leaves forming the rosettes, which are 2 inches across, are roundish, with a red, spiny tip. They are a pale green and covered with a light grey waxy material. The flowers come on stems 3 inches long and are a charming shade of orange-red. Care should be taken not to touch the leaves, or they will be permanently marked and their waxen appearance spoiled. This species is one of the most desirable of the solid-looking Echeverias and much in demand as a house plant. Like *E. glauca,* it is stemless and ideal for a small pot.

*E. elegans* (elegant) is one of the species (among the most attractive) with a texture reminiscent of alabaster, the surface of the leaves being white and glistening, the margins slightly translucent and reddish – a lovely foliage plant for winter decoration. It forms numerous offsets and is thus easily propagated. The leaves are ovalish, concave, rather thick, about an inch long, round at the top and with a tiny but conspicuous point. The flowers are a pretty shade of pink and tipped with yellow. The plant occurs in the State of Hidalgo, in the eastern part of Mexico.

*E. gibbiflora var. metallica* is better known than the type (*gibbiflora* means with flowers swollen on one side); the plants are found south of Mexico City. The variety described here is greatly admired for the metallic sheen of its leaves; they have a fine red edge and are from 5 to 8 inches long and 3 to 5 inches wide, quite large compared with the leaves of most of the other Echeverias we grow indoors. The upper part of the surface is concave and the lower part is keeled at the base. The plant is of shrubby habit; the flowers are scarlet and carried in freely branched clusters.

*E. Harmsii* (named for Dr. H. Harm of the Botanical Museum, Berlin); a species from Mexico, with 12 inch stems carrying rosettes of small narrow leaves (an inch long), pointed and covered with soft hairs. It has unusually attractive flowers, these being bell-shaped, rather large and red with yellow tips. In time *E. Harmsii* makes a beautiful plant for a good-sized pot.

*E. nuda* (*naked; bare*) is another Mexican species with stems, though these are half the length of those of *E. Harmsii;* the rosettes are composed of smallish green leaves, 2 inches long and an inch wide. The flowers are a pretty shade of yellow.

*E. pulvinata* (*cushion-like;* probably referring to the hairy or felted appearance of the rosettes); a popular *Echevaria* from the State of Oaxaca and much admired for its white felted velvety-looking leaves. Its stems are short and branching; the rosettes loose or open and composed of thick leaves, 2 inches long and an inch wide; they are flattish above and have a short point at the apex. The leaves, as they age, become brownish; the brown velvety effect is particularly striking. And the flowers, too, add to the beauty of the plant: they are a brilliant scarlet colour, about ½-inch long, and borne on spreading leafy stems.

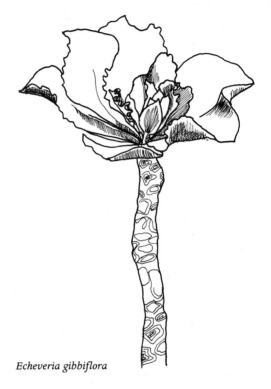

*Echeveria gibbiflora*

*E. setosa* (*bristly;* referring to the foliage); from Puebla in Central Mexico, north of Oaxaca, and considered to be one of the easiest of all the Echeverias to grow indoors. The rosettes are stemless and make plenty of offsets. The rosettes, about 5 inches wide, and composed of leaves, convex on both sides, are narrow, green, and densely covered with white hairs. The flowers are also outstandingly beautiful; they are a bright shining red, tipped with yellow and freely produced. This *Echeveria* will be found in most collections.

162

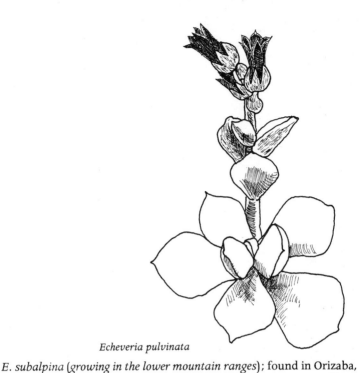

*Echeveria pulvinata*

*E. subalpina* (*growing in the lower mountain ranges*); found in Orizaba, south-east of Puebla; a charming species forming dense rosettes of long narrow brownish-green leaves, tapering toward the base, the largest about 3 inches in length. The lower surfaces are convex, the upper flattish; in full sun the leaves often assume a deep red colour. The flowers are an attractive cinnibar red. This *Echeveria* is sometimes used for edging flower beds, the plants, like *E. glauca,* being lifted in the autumn and wintered in a frost-proof greenhouse. They should not be put out again till about mid-June. Whether grown outdoors or inside, they must be watered regularly throughout the summer months. In winter keep the soil just damp enough to prevent the plants' shrivelling. As already mentioned, Echeverias, like the same sort of soil as Cotyledons – a light, sandy soil does very well.

Although there are hundreds of succulent species of *Euphorbia,* only one is listed in each of the succulents catalogues I have had sent to me by specialists' nurseries. And that is the popular *Euphorbia splendens* – known as the Crown of Thorns. In many florists', however, several different species are offered for sale: recently I came across the following three in a local shop: *Euphorbia globosa; E. meloformis* and *E. pendula,* the last-named was probably a permanent decoration, as the plant was growing in a hanging-basket. The Poinsettia (*E. pulcherrima*) is better known than any of them; but it is not a succulent. The succulent species mostly occur in South Africa. They are all tender plants needing in cultivation a winter temperature round about 50F (10C). Some of them bear a striking resemblance to certain cacti (*E. horrida* looks like one of the Barrel Cacti); they are distinguished from them, however, by having no areoles and by the milky latex which exudes freely when the stems are cut or damaged. Cacti exude a colourless juice. Occasionally one hears them called Milkweeds, occasionally Spurges; and the 'milk' (latex) is acrid and poisonous and will blister sensitive skins if not washed off quickly, and indeed can cause sepsis in scratches and sores.

The usual method of propagation is by cuttings, letting the ends dry for about a week before inserting the pieces in sand or sand and peat-moss (equal quantities of both); they may take months, however, to form roots. Many gardeners prefer to sow seed; and when they do they take the precaution to protect the capsules before they are fully ripe, since they explode and scatter the seed some feet in the air. Like many other genera of succulent plants, Euphorbias hybridise freely; consequently the plants raised by seed taken from collections of different species are not always first-rate. Euphorbias need a perfectly-drained loamy soil containing some coarse sand and leafmould (or a little bone-meal); it should be a richer compost than that used for most cacti. Winter is their resting period; and then they should be kept quite dry; in the growing season they need a fairly moist soil and all the sunlight you can provide. A warm sunny living-room is an excellent place for them.

*E. globosa* (*small and globular;* referring to the roundish clumps of branches); a native of Cape Province. It is an odd-looking plant – grotesque perhaps – rather like a jointed rubber toy representing some animal. It has a short, fleshy, thickish main stem and roundish (sub-globose) growths or branches produced irregularly (that is, at varying intervals up the stem); they grow longer with age and are covered with honeycomb-like tubercles. It is surely one of the oddest-shaped succulents you can grow in a pot. The greenish flowers, like all those of the Euphorbias, are small and insignificant. The colour and decoration is often provided by big showy bracts (petal-like leaves) – the scarlet Poinsettia probably has the showiest. In *E. globosa* the flowers come on 3-inch stalks at the end of the fleshy branches. But apart from the stout woody-like stalks they are scarcely noticeable: the shape of the plant is much more interesting.

*E. horrida* (*very prickly;* referring to the spines on the stem or stems);

this species also occurs in Cape Province and resembles the Barrel Cacti (see Chapter Two, page 42, where the Golden Barrel Cactus is described). In the wild the fat barrel-shaped stem may reach a height of 2 or 3 feet; but plants bought in pots remain small for years. The stem or stems are ribbed – this species often branches freely from the base – young plants have about 7 ribs, but many more when they mature; on the crests of the ribs, which are deeply grooved between, grow spines derived from flower-stalks, often three together. The flowers are inconspicuous. This *Euphorbia* and *E. polygona,* which has fewer spines, are the only natural hosts of the Mistletoe with red berries, *Viscum minimum.*

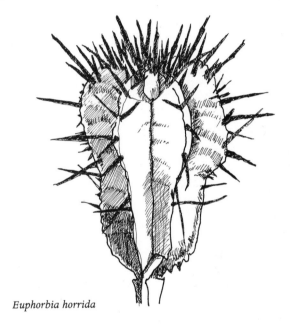

*Euphorbia horrida*

*E. meloformis* (*melon-shaped*) is sometimes called the Melon Spurge and is one of those most useful plants that will live for many years in a small pot. It is another species from Cape Province. Being dwarf and never more than about 3 inches wide it is popular with collectors who have a limited amount of room for their plants. After some years additional globular stems appear round the base. These stems or plant-bodies (wider than they are tall) grow from a long turnip-like tap-root; they are grey-green in colour, glossy, and have 8 ribs, deeply furrowed or grooved between. They are sometimes banded purple. *E. meloformis* has tiny insignificant flowers on long, branched stalks, and is one of the spineless kinds.

*E. pendula* (*hanging;* referring to the stems); a many-branched species from Cape Province; the long, hanging stems are cylindrical, $\frac{1}{4}$-inch thick, forked and divided into 2-inch-long segments. It is naturally suited to a hanging-basket and is among the toughest and longest-lived of the tender succulents grown for indoor decoration. The colour of the stems is a pleasing shade of mat green.

*E. splendens* (*splendid*) is called by some collectors *E. millii,* a specific name which has priority over the other, since *E. millii* was first used for this species by Des Moulin in 1826, three years before the name *E. splendens* appeared. It is a spiny succulent shrub and grows up to 3 feet high. The flowers are scarlet and showy and come in forked clusters at the end of reddish stalks which are sticky or clammy. The leaves, thin and bright green, are narrowly oval and grow only at the ends of the shoots. They fall during a long dry spell and the plant isn't much to look at then, apart from its brown, furrowed, branching stems with their long, tapering spines. This *Euphorbia* is an early flowerer and needs, when the buds begin to show red, a temperature of about 55F (13C). In winter it is best kept in a warm room and should be given a little tepid water now and then just to keep the soil from drying out completely. *E. splendens* is a native of South Madagascar.

Finally I am describing a species which I have seen only in collections: this is *E. obesa* (*succulent*). It is an astonishing plant, 'looking', according to one grower, 'as though it had been blown up, balloon-shape, and then painted over with purple and green stripes.' Its round sculptured stem and its grey-green surface ornamented with longitudinal and transverse purple lines make it one of the most beautiful of all the tender species in cultivation. It is a pity it is so difficult to get. It is a native of Cape Province and has a ribbed, globose stem or plant-body up to about 8 inches high; the ribs (8 in number) are not prominent, and the furrows between are not deep. *E. obesa,* like *E. meloformis* and many of the succulent species, is unisexual; that is, there are male and female plants; I have seen both in bloom together; and both male and female flowers are small and insignificant. Most of the succulent Euphorbias are prized of course for their curious, and often very beautiful, shapes. This particular *Euphorbia* revels in dry conditions; even in hot summer weather it doesn't want too much water and in winter the soil may be allowed to become desert-dry.

The genus belongs to the *Family Euphorbiaceae.* And the generic name is said to commemorate a physician of the name of Euphorbus who lived at the beginning of the Christian era. King Juba 11 of Mauritania (the old name of a North African region) discovered the plant growing on, or in the vicinity of Mount Atlas in North Africa. The plant is thought to have been *E. resinifera* (*resinous*) and to have valuable medicinal properties. The king was an erudite man and highly extolled the virtues of the plant in a treatise he published entitled *De Euphorbia Herba*.

*Faucaria:* only one or two plants appear in catalogues. There are not more than about a dozen species altogether described by botanists and some were at one time (like *Cheiridopsis,* page 152; and *Conophytum,* page 153) included in *Mesembryanthemum.* Occasionally one comes across the plants labelled with this name. *Faucaria* is from *fauces,* throat – the gaping leaves resemble an open mouth. They are dwarf, nearly stemless, tender succulents, classed with the other Mimicry plants but less deserving of the name perhaps than, say, the *Lithops* and *Gibbaeum,* which are often undistinguishable from the stones and pebbles among which they grow. Many of the plants offered by florists are hybrids and simply labelled *Faucaria;* in some cases *Mesembryanthemum.*

*Faucaria* are characterised by the long prominent teeth on the edges of the leaves, which are joined at the base. These teeth are so distinct on the wide-open leaves that the plants are known as Tiger's Chaps (jaws or chops) or Cat's Chaps, names not much used, however, nowadays. Many of the leaves are keeled or boat-shaped and the flowers are large, usually yellow, stalkless and open as a rule in the afternoon.

*Faucaria felina* (cat-toothed, probably; referring to the toothed jaw-like leaves); a species resembling *F. tigrina* (*tiger-toothed*), but having fewer and smaller teeth. The leaves, pale green in colour, are 2 inches long and often turn red as they age. There are whitish spots on the surface (less conspicuous though than in *F. tigrina*); the teeth along the edges are recurved and fleshy and number from 3 to 5. The flowers are yellow and measure about 2 inches across. The plant sometimes carries two and they bloom together. Like the other species, *F. felina* comes from the Karroo, the name given to a barren tract of table-land 2000 to 3000 feet above sea-level in South Africa, with heavy clay soil, which however bursts into blossom when the rains come.

*F. lupina* (*wolf-like*) I have seen only in collections. Its leaves are $1\frac{1}{2}$ inches long, flat above, convex on the under side and keeled toward the apex. The teeth, 7 to 9, often taper to fine bristles; and the flowers (aster-shaped like those of the other species) are yellow and solitary (grow singly) and on the small side.

*F. tigrina* has rather bigger leaves, which are thick and turgid-looking – as though swollen with a superabundance of juice – they are 2 inches long and an inch wide at the base and have about 10 strong recurved teeth, which taper to fine bristles. The leaves are grey-green in colour and covered with white dots. Teeth and keel (boat-shaped end of leaf) are cartilaginous or gristle-like and in strong sunlight show a pinkish tinting. The flowers – often two together – are 2 inches wide and an attractive shade of golden-yellow. But this *Faucaria* is worth growing for its foliage alone: the crowded, succulent leaves soon fill a small pot and are decorative at all times. The new leaves are closed with the teeth interlocking (as in all the species), and spread wide open as they grow and develop. Faucarias should be rested from December to April and during that period need very little water. The growing season is summer. Propagation is usually by cuttings, or by division of old plants.

*Gasteria verrucosa*

*Gasteria,* like *Aloe,* belong to the *Family Liliaceae* and rather resemble the *Aloe;* they are distinguished from them, however, by the shape and form of the flowers: those of Aloes are bell-shaped; in Gasteria they are swollen at the base – *Gasteria* is from *gaster,* belly or stomach; the flowers are said to resemble the shape of the stomach. The leaves, thick and succulent, are mostly two-ranked and, as the plants age, often form rosettes. The inflorescence (flower-cluster) is from 2 to 3 feet long and may be branched; the flowers themselves are pendent and a shade of red or reddish-orange. All the species are natives of

South Africa and occasionally one comes across them labelled Aloe, which is now a synonym. Gasterias are grown in the same way as Aloes.

G. *verrucosa* (*warty;* referring to the numerous white warts or tubercles on the leaves); this appears to be the best known of the plants offered for sale and it has produced several hybrids. It is a tufted plant (leaves growing together at the base), with its dull grey-green leaves in two ranks. They are from 4 to 6 inches long, ½-inch wide and covered with white tubercles (or warts) which make the leaves very rough to the touch. In shape they are concave, with sharp tapering ends. The flowers, red, are carried on branched stems, 2 feet or so tall. This is an excellent choice for townspeople who have only a limited amount of room for their plants; it does well in a window facing north, since it prospers in semi-shade; and it remains small for many years and seldom needs repotting. Propagate it by planting out some of the offsets which form round the parent plant.

*Gibbaeum* were at one time included in *Mesembryanthemum* and belong to the same family as does that genus, viz. *Aizoaceae;* and we grow these plants as we do the other Mimicry Mesembryanthemums – *Conophytum*, for instance (page 154). The generic name is from *gibba*, a hump; the fat succulent leaves grow in pairs, and one is always prolonged into a hump: *G. dispar* and *G. pubescens* are good illustrations of this leaf character. It has been said that in some species the leaves in profile resemble a shark's head, the lower, smaller, leaf being the jaw, and the split between the leaves the mouth. *Gibbaeum*, like *Faucaria*, come from the Karroo. *G. album* (white) is one of the most attractive, with stemless plant-bodies formed by two unequal leaves; the plant-bodies, green, covered with minute white hairs, are an inch long and about ¾-inch wide. The cleft or split is at first scarcely visible, but as the plant grows it soon begins to widen and open. The flowers, which arise out of the opening, are white, aster-like, an inch across and have very short stalks. On mature clumps both white and purplish flowers are sometimes produced. The new leaves begin to form next to the flower-buds and expand and grow as the old plant-body withers and dies. This species is said to be rather difficult in cultivation. But if the plant is rested and water withheld during the summer (from June to the end of October), it will thrive and start blooming at the end of the year; the flowers continue to bloom till February, and then fade. (The soil should be a sandy gritty loam, the surface round the plant being sprinkled with small pebbles or flints).

G. *Heathii*, on the other hand, blooms in the spring and must be rested from July to February. No water is given to this plant during the winter months. *G. Heathii* – reputedly the most difficult of all the Gibbaeums – is stemless, like *G. album*, and also forms clumps. The plant-bodies, greyish-green, are almost round, about an inch in height, the pair of leaves (forming them) being hemispherical and remaining close together – the cleft or split is at the top and from it grows the pinkish flowers and the new pair of leaves. (*G. Heathii* commemorates Dr. Rodier Heath, d. 1940, a well-known collector of succulent plants.) Specialists who grow these species state that overwatering the plants does more damage than anything else. They like a bright, sunny position – are in fact ideal cool greenhouse plants – and the winter blooming kinds should be stood in their pots in containers plunged in ashes mixed with coarse sand, which is watered when the plants begin to make new growth and are coming into flower. Direct watering (into the pots) is thus avoided. Propagation is by seeds or cuttings.

*Greenovia* is a genus of four species, all native to the Canary Islands, where they flourish in stony mountainous regions. They are often found growing in crevices and seem to appreciate the shelter of overhanging rocks and stones. The genus belongs to the Crassula Family, *Crassulaceae;* and the generic name commemorates George Bellas Greenough (1778–1855), English geologist. Only one species is offered by nurseries – *Greenovia aurea*, said to be the most attractive of the four. It occurs often at high altitudes, up to 5000 feet, in the mountains, and, like the other species, resembles *Sempervivum* in habit, forming rosettes which expand during growth. *G. aurea* (*golden;* referring to the colour of the flowers) has blue-green leaves, which turn pink during the resting period. They are broad at the base and the apex (the largest 4 inches long), fleshy, with thin transparent edges; and they form a rosette with a cup-like hollow centre and they open wide when growth commences. The flowers, golden-yellow, are carried in clusters at the end of an erect leafy stem, 12 inches or so long. Those who have seen this plant growing in its natural habitat say it is at its loveliest in a quiescent condition when the rosettes become urn-shaped and glow deep pink in the centre. It is a fairly hardy plant and doesn't mind a coldish room in winter. A light gritty loam is ideal for it; and it is usually increased by offsets.

*Haworthias,* like *Gasterias,* are closely related to the Aloes; and, like the Gasterias, are distinguished from Aloes in the character of the flowers, these being two-lipped. The two species described here are stemless – some have a short stem, or stems 4 to 6 inches long. *Haworthia attenuata* (*narrowing to a point; attenuated*) forms a rosette and produces plenty of offsets; the leaves are slender, tapering, thick and fleshy; small white tubercles decorate the upper part, and on the back they are arranged in conspicuous horizontal lines. The flowers, greenish-white, come on slender stems and, like those of the other species, are not particularly attractive. Haworthias are all native to South Africa.

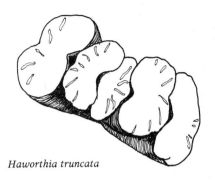

*Haworthia truncata*

*H. truncata* (*cut off square;* referring to the tops of the leaves) is one of the so-called 'window' plants (these are succulents that grow practically buried in the desert sand and get what light they require through the translucent tips of the leaves, which are exposed to the hot sun). The leaves of *H. truncata* are 2-ranked, dull green and have flattened translucent tops, which admit light to the chlorophyll-tissue within. Haworthias need a sunny position in a room that has a temperature in winter of about 40F (5C). In summer they should be stood outside if possible and protected from the blazing sun and sheltered from heavy rain. A cold frame in a shady place would be ideal for them. During a wet spell simply draw up the 'lights' (the glazed, sliding cover) over the plants. Grow them in a compost of good heavy loam (one part) and a second part of equal quantities of powdered leafmould and coarse sand. Repot the plants every second year, since the thick fleshy roots die off annually and rot, and consequently make the soil sour. Propagation is usually by removing some of the offsets and growing them on in sandy soil.

*Kalanchoe* are tender succulent plants native mostly to Tropical and South Africa; some occur in China and in regions extending south to the Malay Peninsula; some in Madagascar, Arabia, India; and one species occurs in Tropical America. They belong to the Crassula Family, *Crassulaceae,* and are closely related to *Bryophyllum,* which genus was at one time included in *Kalanchoe;* but the structure of the flowers distinguishes the two genera; furthermore, plantlets aren't normally formed on the leaves in *Kalanchoe* as they are in *Bryophyllum.*

*Kalanchoe beharensis* comes from Behara in Madagascar and has greenish-brown stems about 2 feet tall. Stems and leaves are both covered with soft reddish velvety hair, in their young state, then the

171

colour turns grey-white as the plant matures; eventually the leaves become quite smooth. They are thick, fleshy and very attractive (5 to 8 inches long), triangular and wavy along the edges; the entire surface, too, becomes wavy as the leaf develops, which rather obscures its true triangular shape. The old stems are characteristically knotted and the leaf-scars (made by fallen leaves) are conspicuous. But the plant produces no flowers in cultivation. And those that do appear in the wild are small and unattractive. Like many tender greenhouse succulents, this Kalanchoe is essentially a foliage plant and, like quite a few succulents, it needs a warm atmosphere in winter (temperature not below 50F (10C)). It should be given a little water now and then, otherwise the beautiful head of leaves will begin to droop and some of the leaves fall. It needs a deep leafy well-drained loam. After some years, when the plants get tall, the tops are cut off and used as cuttings. They soon strike in sandy soil and provide new plants.

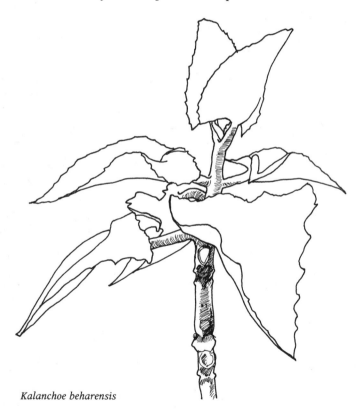

*Kalanchoe beharensis*

*K. Blossfeldiana* (commemorating Robert Blossfeld, cactus dealer of Potsdam, a suburb of Berlin): a species from Madagascar, and a favourite house plant in many countries. It has produced a number of charming hybrids; and these, when treated artificially – by reducing the amount of summer sunlight – will bloom in winter. (The plants I have seen in different collections bloomed about March.) The flowers, a brilliant scarlet, are carried in small heads or clusters. The hybrids, however, bear flowers of various colours. This *Kalanchoe* is a small shrubby plant with numerous stems that reach a height of 10 or 12 inches; the leaves, dark green and ovalish (3 inches long and $1\frac{1}{2}$ inches wide) have red marginal lines and are wavy at the edge. The plant is easily raised from seed planted in heat in February. Like the other species, it needs plenty of water through the growing season.

*K. marmorata* (*marbled; mottled;* referring to the colouring of the leaves) comes from Eritrea and Abyssinia, and is regarded by collectors as the most beautiful of the species obtainable. It is a slow grower and has roundish, sessile (stemless) leaves, about 4 inches wide; the base colouring is green with grey-blue waxy coating, which is marked with reddish-brown flecks; if set among some kinds of similarly-coloured marble-chippings the leaves would be difficult to see. The flowers, seldom seen in cultivation, are white and about 3 inches long. *K. marmorata* is a magnificent succulent for a pot and well worth all the care and attention you can give it. It needs a perfectly-drained sandy loam containing plenty of powdered peat or leafmould, and should be kept in a sunny place, in a room where the temperature does not fall below 50F (10C). The soil must not be allowed to dry out completely.

*K. tomentosa* (*densely woolly*) a native of Madagascar and sometimes labelled *Kalanchoe madagascariensis*, a name no longer used. The whole plant is hairy; the stem, ultimately 18 inches long, branches from the base and is covered with whitish-grey hairs. The leaves, stalkless and narrow ($1\frac{1}{2}$ inches long and $\frac{3}{4}$-inch wide) come in a rosette at the top of the stem; they are convex on the upper surface, and the margins rounded; the felt-like hairs on the tips are rust-red and turn deep brown as the leaves mature and age. Flowers are not found on cultivated plants. This is a choice succulent, and a favourite with collectors. Its silvery plush-like stems and leaves make it one of the most arresting of all the foliage plants we can grow indoors.

There are over 100 species of *Kalanchoe*, but only one or two are offered by the nurseries; those I have described here are among the loveliest, and are the best for indoor cultivation. The word *Kalanchoe*, by the way, is from the Chinese name of one of the species.

*Kleinia* were at one time included in *Senecio;* both genera belong to the Daisy Family, *Compositae;* these succulents (*Kleinia*) are all tender house plants and occur mostly in Tropical and South Africa. They are easy to grow in pots; they need a compost of loam, leafmould and sharp sand, and a winter temperature of 45F (7C).

*Kleinia articulata (jointed)* is the best known and often the only species listed by nurseries. It has smooth, cylindrical, jointed stems (the joints are about 6 inches long and $\frac{1}{2}$ inch thick) of a glaucous blue colour, which carry in winter pale green fleshy lobed leaves. (The popular name, by the way, is Candle Plant.) This is an exceptional easy species to grow. It needs plenty of moisture in the growing season and only a light watering when it is resting. The flowers, which have an unpleasant smell, come in cylindric heads and are yellow; they are usually in full bloom about January. (There is in cultivation a variety, with much shorter and much rounder joints, which will live for years in a very small pot.)[1] *K. articulata* is a native of South Africa. It is easily propagated by cuttings – allow the cut surfaces to dry first, before inserting the pieces in the soil.

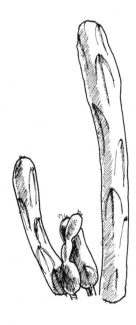

*Kleinia articulata*

*K. gomphophylla (gomphos,* club or bolt; *phyllon,* leaf; referring to the globular-shape of the leaf), a native of South West Africa, with extra-ordinary leaves, shaped rather like a gooseberry. They are $\frac{3}{4}$-inch long, sharply pointed and veined; the veins or stripes are translucent and

[1] The plant is probably *Kleinia articulata var. globosus,* often listed as a *Senecio.*

allow the light to reach the centre of the leaf. Bright sunshine shows up very remarkably this beautiful veining. The plant needs a pan so that its creeping stems can develop easily and root as they grow in the soil.

*K. neriifolia* (*Oleander-leaved* – lance-shaped) comes from the Canary Isles where it grows into a shrubby plant 3 feet or so tall. In a pot it remains small for many years and is admired chiefly for its thick grey-green rugged-looking stem covered with white leaf-scars. The largest leaves are about 6 inches long and $\frac{1}{2}$-inch wide, greyish in colour and have a prominent central vein; they come in whorls or tufts at the end of the stems (branching from the main stem) and fall in the spring. The plant is rested through the summer months and kept reasonably dry during that time. In autumn the yellowish-white flowers, carried in loose clusters, begin to open and are at their best in November: like the other succulent Kleinias, it is easily increased by cuttings.

*K. repens* (*creeping*) is a species from Cape Province, with the lower portions of its stems creeping or growing below soil level. The upright stems usually reach a height of 12 inches or so and carry narrow fleshy glaucous blue leaves, which are grooved above and have a small tip. The flowers are white and come in flattish heads in summer. It is a charming little succulent for a small pot and easily increased by cuttings.

*K. tomentosa* (*densely woolly*: the plant is entirely covered with close pure white wool), a native of South Africa and a valuable succulent for a pot, being of neat habit and attractive at all times of the year. The leaves are cylindrical (rather like peanuts or monkey-nuts in shape); they are tapered at both ends, about $1\frac{1}{2}$ inches long and $\frac{1}{2}$-inch thick; they have very short stalks and come in clusters on fleshy stems which ultimately reach a height of 10 inches or so. The flowers are an attractive shade of orange-yellow and bloom in July. The plant should be kept reasonably dry through the winter months.

The genus was named in honour of Jacob Theodor Klein (1685–1759), a German botanist.

*Lithops* are the Pebble plants, treasured by collectors of succulents for their resemblance to small smooth round stones or pebbles – they are like *Conophytum* (page 153) and often difficult to distinguish from the stones which surround them. It is said that the colouring of some of the species is affected by the stones among which they grow in the wild – they are natives of hot sunny places in Namaqualand, South Africa. As in *Conophytum,* the new plant-body (or pair of leaves) is formed within the old one; this eventually withers and becomes a mere dried-up skin. The flowers, some of which are delightfully fragrant, are stemless and arise from within the cleft or fissure at the top of the plant. They are usually white or yellow (never red or pink) and are rather like miniature asters.

*Lithops* were at one time grouped with *Mesembryanthemum;* but the latter name now appears only as a synonym; and, like *Mesembryanthemum,* the genus belongs to the *Family Aizoaceae.* The generic name is from the Greek *lithos,* stone; and *ops,* appearance . . .

*Lithops bella* (pretty) is a species which forms clumps of 5 or 6 plant-bodies, each body being about an inch tall and brownish-yellow in colour (the plants resemble the granite pebbles surrounding them in their habitats). People who have seen this Lithops growing in the wild say that despite the camouflage small reptiles will often ferret the plants out and devour them. The upper surface is convex and has dark brown moss-like markings. The flowers, an inch wide, are white and bloom in early autumn; the plant is rested through the winter and early spring and given no water during that period. Another species, *L. lericheana,* often found growing near *L. bella,* has white flowers which are sweetly scented.

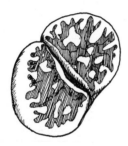

*Lithops bella*

*L. Fulleri, L. Julii* and *L. optica* also have white flowers; the last-mentioned is popular with collectors and forms clumps; the plant-bodies, an inch tall, have a deep cleft across the upper surface which widens as the plants grow, and from the openings arise the daisy-like flowers and then the new growths. This upper surface is grey to yellow-ish-brown in colour, with the tips translucent to admit the light – like some of the other *Lithops,* it is a 'window' or 'windowed' plant. (I have occasionally come across this species labelled *Mesembryanthemum opticum.*) Another 'windowed' species is *L. pseudotruncatella,* which has obconical plant-bodies (cone-shaped, but inverted) with a shallow fissure running completely across the top surface. The translucent area is ornamented with a network of veins and tiny dots. This species has charming yellow daisy-like flowers, which are in full bloom in September. The specific epithet means closely-resembling (*pseudo*) the species formerly called *Mesembryanthemum truncatellum*. These *Lithops* are easily propagated by seeds or by cuttings.

*Mesembryanthemum* is a large group of plants containing a few hardy species, (hardy enough in a warm area, that is) and many tender plants, all of which must be grown indoors or under glass. Some of the Mimicry plants, that were once listed as Mesembryanthemums, have already been described – see *Cheiridopsis, Conophytum, Faucaria, Gibbaeum, Lithops*.

The new generic names determine the arrangement of the following plants – *Bergeranthus; Carruanthus;* etc., *Mesembryanthemum (Bergeranthus) multiceps (with many heads)* a native of Cape Province, a stemless succulent with charming daisy-like yellow flowers, an inch across, and red on the outside; they bloom in July and open in the late afternoon. The leaves come in small, dense rosettes; they are a shade of fresh green, up to 2 inches in length, triangular and recurved toward the tip, which is often furnished with a tiny bristle. The upper surface is flat, the lower bluntly keeled. As the plant suckers freely it is quite easily increased by division.

*M. scapiger (scape-bearing)* resembles *M. multiceps,* but the leaves of the former plant are twice as long and a darker shade of green. One leaf of each pair in the rosette is shorter than the other, the longer leaf being keeled, and both edged with a lighter-coloured horny or bony tissue. The flowers, 2 inches across, are golden-yellow, reddish outside, and come in profusion all through the summer. Both species are described by many botanists under the genus *Bergeranthus* and are often labelled with this name. Both plants are best kept on the dry side at all times; if put outside in a frame during the hot summer weather the framelights must be pulled up over them at night and always during a rainy spell. They may be kept in the same pot for years and really prefer a soil on the poor side – certainly not containing any kind of fertiliser or stimulants. The temperature in winter in the room where they are kept should not rise above 45F (7C) but frost must be excluded.

*M. (Carruanthus) caninum (pertaining to dogs)*. The specific epithet seems an inapposite one, though it has been suggested that it refers to the toothed leaves. The term is used mostly, however, to describe flowers, the scentless kinds being considered inferior (*caninum*). The plant is a native of South Africa and is a short-stemmed species, with erect leaves which form clumps. The leaves are grey-green, $2\frac{1}{2}$ inches long and have toothed edges. The upper surface is flat, the underside convex and keeled. During the winter, when the plant is resting, the shape of the leaf alters slightly, the upper surface becoming somewhat concave, and the toothing more prominent, the plant then rather resembling a *Faucaria* (see page 167). The flowers, carried on stalks up to 4 inches long, are yellow and shaded red on the outside. This plant, sometimes listed as *Carruanthus caninum,* is cultivated like *M. multiceps* (*Bergeranthus,* page 177).

*M. hispidum* (*bristly*): like the other Mesembryanthemums I am describing here this plant has been given another specific name by many botanists and collectors. And the name (*Drosanthemum hispidum*) may appear on the label of plants sent out by the nurseries. Several of these Mesembryanthemums are grouped together under this name and they are all ideal plants for the amateur and the indoor gardener, for they have no special cultural requirements. The soil should be an ordinary sandy loam (rather on the thin side in fact), which promotes plenty of flowering growths. Too rich a soil always results in the plants producing foliage at the expense of flowers. This species is attractive at all times of the year; the flowers, deep purple or magenta, and freely produced, are an inch wide and carried in threes on the stems; the foliage, with its grey-white hairs, is ornamental at all times. The stems are longish (often 2 feet) and in time begin to trail over the side of the pot or pan in which the plant is grown. It is most effective grown in a hanging basket; when the flowers fade, the brownish stems and cylindrical leaves (an inch long), green and turning red in full sun, are delightful. Three other species closely related to *M. hispidum* are *M. candens,* with small white flowers; *M. floribundum,* with pale pink flowers nearly an inch wide; and the most beautiful of them, I think, *M. speciosum,* whose flowers are 2 inches wide and have deep orange petals and green centres. All these species are natives of Cape Province; and they are often labelled *Drosanthemum.*

*M. aurantiacum* (*orange-coloured*) is also from Cape Province and another easy *Mesembryanthemum* to grow, either in a pot indoors, or as a summer bedding plant. This species, like *M. hispidum,* has longish brown slender stems. They are erect and carry inch-long, grey-green leaves, three-angled and furnished with a spiny tip. The surfaces are roughened and have translucent dots. Its gorgeous glowing orange flowers are its great attraction. They are borne in profusion all through the summer and much valued for the bright splash of colour they provide indoors or in the garden. *M. aureum* (*golden*) is similar and is also from Cape Province. The leaves are larger (up to 2 inches long) and pruinose, or frosty-looking; and the flowers, although not so striking (golden-yellow) are larger: up to $2\frac{1}{2}$ inches in diameter. It prospers well in a pot and may be left undisturbed for several years. Both these species are described by many writers under the genus (*Lampranthus*) and are often labelled with this name.

*M. deltoides* (*triangular*; referring to the leaves, which are shaped like the Greek letter $\Delta$, *delta*); it has smallish pink flowers which are almond-scented and bloom from spring to summer. It is a compact-growing *Mesembryanthemum*, with reddish much-branched stems, the shoots of which carry attractive grey-green pruinose leaves $\frac{3}{4}$-inch long, triangular in shape, bent inward, and furnished with red-coloured teeth along the edges. The silvery, frosted, look of the foliage makes this *Mesembryanthemum* attractive all through the year. Like all the other plants described here, it is easy to grow and a good flowering succulent for a pot. It must be kept quite dry during its resting period, which is late autumn and winter, and it needs only a little water even when growing and flowering. *M. deltoides* is now listed by most writers as *Oscularia deltoides*. There are apparently very few species included in this new genus. *M. caulescens* (*Oscularia*) has triangular fleshy leaves and small scented pink flowers; and a variety of *M. deltoides* (*Oscularia*), viz. *Var. muricatum,* is very like the type plant but smaller.

*Monanthes* is a genus of 10 species and belongs to the *Crassula* family, *Crassulaceae*. The plants occur in the Canary Islands, The Salvage Islands and Morocco. The very pretty winter-blooming *Monanthes muralis* (*growing on walls*), a native of the Canary Islands, is tender and should be grown in a small pot and housed in a frost-proof room or a greenhouse. It is a shrubby, perennial plant, about $3\frac{1}{2}$ inches high, with tiny fleshy very thick leaves ($\frac{1}{4}$ inch long and $\frac{1}{8}$ inch wide), spotted purple, carried at the end of brown branches or stems, and it has dainty, star-like white flowers marked with pinkish-red, which come in clusters of 3 or more. This is a really enchanting little succulent and at its best in late winter – it has a long flowering period. Two other species not so easily obtainable are *M. anagensis* (*of the Anaga Mountains, Canary Islands*), which has numerous small branches about 6 inches high, bearing fat, juicy leaves (almost cylindrical) an inch long, green and occasionally marked with red. They are bunched together on the stems and are the plant's chief attraction. The flowers, greenish-yellow and blooming in May, are small and insignificant. The other species (also from the Canary Islands) is *M. polyphylla* (with many leaves). In the wild this little succulent grows in the crevices of damp rocks, sending out creeping stems of minute pale green, very fleshy, juicy leaves in rosettes. The flowers, $\frac{1}{2}$-inch across, are purplish, like tiny parasols, and bloom in early summer.

*Monanthes* are cultivated like Crassulas and Cotyledons (page 155); but they seem to prosper in quite cool rooms during the winter months, and in partial shade during the hot summer weather. *M. muralis* flourishes in fairly light sandy soils and needs only 'mist' spraying in the summer. Too much water will cause the flowers to damp off. Keep this choice little succulent reasonably dry at all times. The generic name is misleading: *mono,* one; and *anthos,* flower: botanists wrongly thought the flowers to be solitary, i.e. appear singly.

*Pachyphytum* is a genus of about eight species and closely related to *Echeveria,* and like that genus belongs to the *Crassula Family*. But the former have very thick succulent leaves which are arranged in open rosettes: Echeverias usually have compact rosettes, with much thinner leaves. *Pachyphytum* were at one time included in *Cotyledon* and are cultivated like those plants. They are best kept permanently indoors and when watering them avoid wetting the leaves, otherwise the silvery-white waxy covering will be spoiled. (This covering consists of glistening frost-like particles.) The generic name is from *pachys,* thick; and *phytos,* plant; the leaves are very thick and juicy.

*Pachyphytum brachteosum* (*with conspicuous bracts*) is found in Mexico, like the other species. A mature specimen has thick brownish stems up to 10 inches tall and very attractive glistening white (pruinose) leaves; they are thick and fleshy, 3 to 4 inches long, an inch wide, with rounded margins and curve upward slightly. The flowers, bright red, are $\frac{3}{4}$-inch long, the sepals (leaf-like case of flower-bud) longer than the petals. The flowering period is April and May.

*P. Hookeri* (in honour of Sir W. J. Hooker, 1785–1865; or of his son Sir J. D. Hooker, both famous English experts). This species grows taller than the preceding – up to 2 feet – but unfortunately for those who grow it in a pot indoors it remains small for many years. The thick grey-green succulent leaves are at first crowded on the stem but become more widely spaced as the plant matures and gets taller. They are cylindrical, about an inch long, slightly flattened on the upper surface and have a palish tip. The flowers are bright red and tipped with yellow. When the plant gets too tall, say 18 inches or so, the top is removed and used as a cutting.

*P. oviferum* (*egg-shaped;* referring to the leaves) is one of the loveliest succulents one can grow in a pot. The dense white coating on the leaves gives the plant a curiously artificial look – as though it had been moulded out of some soft glowing white substance. It grows slowly, is ideal for a small pot, and has short stems with roughly egg-shaped leaves $1\frac{1}{2}$ inches long, which are sometimes pink-tinted. The flowers, which bloom in early summer, are a charming shade of red. The plant must be watered carefully: use a tiny can with a long narrow spout that will carry the water straight to the soil and not touch the plant itself.

*P. pachyphytoides* is thought to be a garden hybrid between *P. bracteosum* and *Echeveria gibbiflora metallica* and in its dormant state resembles the former plant. The flowers, a charming shade of pink, are freely produced and carried in a long branched inflorescence.

180

These three species are the most popular. *P. werdermannii* is a dwarf species not more than 9 inches tall after many years' growth. It has greyish, silvery-looking leaves, oval in shape, flat above and rounded below and often tinged with pink when exposed to bright sunshine for any length of time. The flowers are white and red.

*Pleiospilos* are Mimicry plants and were at one time grouped with Mesembryanthemums (*Family Aizoaceae*). Like many of the Mimicry plants they are often indistinguishable from the stones and pebbles among which they grow – they are found in Cape Province. The generic name is from *pleios,* full; and *spilos,* spot; the leaves are conspicuously spotted with dark dots. The natural growth (found in many Mimicry plants) consists of a plant-body or one or two pairs of leaves; these are united at the base; they are wide, very thick and often hemispherical.

*Pachyphytum oviferum*

*P. Bolusii* (commemorating Mr. Harry Bolus, 1834–1911, a writer on the Flora of South Africa). The plant-body or growth consists of one pair of brownish-green hemispherical leaves, with dark spots; and without the flowers they much resemble two pieces of granite, broader than they are long – this species has in fact been called the acme of

181

mimicry. The flowers, 2 or 3 inches across, golden-yellow in colour, arise from the centre of each pair of leaves and bring the plant to life. There are usually one to four from each growth and they measure 3 inches across. All *Pleiospilos* grow from May to July and flower during the late summer and autumn. When the new leaves are fully developed watering should cease. Occasionally, when water is given during the winter months, more than one pair of leaves is produced; the plants are then best grown in a wide-topped pan, where they can spread more easily.

*P. simulans* (*imitating*) is a perfect example of a mimicry plant, for its leaves look like pieces of granite. This species much resembles the other, except that the leaves (brownish-green and dotted) are rather larger and wide-opened and are pressed against the soil or detritus (pebbles, stones) in which the plant grows; the tips of the leaves are usually recurved. The flowers are very fine: large, yellow and delicately scented; they come on short stalks, often singly, but occasionally in groups of four.

Two species I have seen in collections and also in florists' are *P. dekenahi* and *P. magnipunctatus* – one collector had both species labelled *Mesembryanthemum*. The first has long, waxy-looking, prui-nose leaves; the second very thick succulent leaves tapering to a point and glaucous-green in colour. *Pleiospilos* are easily raised from seeds.

*Portulacaria* consists of a single species called *P. afra*. The generic name is adapted from *Portulaca*, a closely-related genus; both genera belong to the Purslane family, *Portulaceae*. Some nurseries also list a variegated form and Haage in his CACTI AND SUCCULENTS mentions forms with leaves of varying size and also a mottled-leaved variety, which is probably identical with *P. afra variegata*. *P. afra* sometimes reaches 20 feet. It is rarely seen in collections and doesn't come in for much praise; but it makes an attractive pot-plant and in the course of years grows only very slowly, consequently it seldom needs repotting. In nature it forms dense thickets, and animals feed on its juicy succulent leaves. Like some of the hardier cacti – Opuntias, for instance – it has been utilised for hedging in tropical and sub-tropical countries. It is one of those very useful plants which are both decorative and utili-tarian. The plant produces a maze of branches carrying thick roundish glossy green leaves, the largest being $\frac{3}{4}$-inch long. The flowers are tiny and inconspicuous, a washy pink and come on short, slender stems.

*P. afra variegata* has leaves variegated with yellow and seems to be even much rarer than the type – this, by the way, was introduced into Britain from South Africa about 1730. Portulacarias need a light sandy loam and protection from frost. Keep the soil moderately dry all through the winter months and never overwater the plants. They are easily propagated by cuttings; small side shoots are used, first allowed to 'dry', then inserted in a sandy rooting compost in a heated greenhouse.

*Rochea coccinea*

*Rochea* is a genus of four succulents which occur in South Africa. The name commemorates Daniel de la Roche (1743–1813), a physician and writer, and his son François de la Roche (1782–1814) who was also a physician and a well-known botanist. *Rochea* are closely related to *Crassula* but differ from them chiefly in the shape of the flowers, the corolla in *Rochea* being tubular. Both genera belong to the *Crassulaceae* family. *Rochea coccinea* (*scarlet*) is by far the best known species. The leaves (like those of the other plants) are leathery but not very succulent; they are joined at the base, bright green in colour, small and narrow, and closely set in four rows up the stem, which usually reaches a height of 12 inches or so. The great attraction of the plant is the large flat truss or head of scarlet flowers which have a scent reminiscent of hyacinths. Each tiny flower has four petals at the end of a long tube. The plant is in full bloom during the summer months and is probably the flowering succulent more often seen in florists' windows than any other. Nurserymen, who sell large quantities of this charming plant, insert four or five cuttings in a 3-inch pot of sandy soil and when they are well rooted transfer the whole lot to a 5-inch pot to ensure a mass of flower-heads. Horticulturists have produced several fine varieties or cultivars, two of the best known being *R. coccinea 'flore-Albo'*, with white flowers; and *R. coccinea 'Bicolor'*, red and white. They are of compact habit and make very desirable house plants. These Rocheas are easy plants to grow: in winter keep them in a sunny coolish room (temperature about 45F (7C)); water copiously during the growing season and when the plants are coming into bloom, but in winter only very occasionally – just enough to keep the soil from drying out completely. The three other species of *Rochea* are seldom seen in cultivation: *R. jasminea* (*with jasmine-like flowers*) has flowers which are at first white then turn pinkish-red in late summer; its stems are prostrate and leafy – a good plant (when you can get it) for a hanging-basket; *R. odoratissima* has yellow or pink flowers; and *R. versicolor* (*variously coloured*) is about the same height as *R. coccinea;* it produces a tallish stem crowded with small leathery green leaves and has flat clusters of pink, white or yellow flowers, often red on the outside. All Rocheas are best propagated by cuttings, which are usually taken after the flowering period. Rocheas may also be raised from seeds; but it is many years before one gets sizeable plants that will flower.

*Sansevieria* are grown for their striking leaves, which are thick, fleshy or gristly, tough-looking and mostly sword-shaped. There are about 50 different species, natives of Tropical and South Africa and the East Indies. Not more than half-a-dozen, however, are seen in collections and they all require a minimum winter temperature of 55F (13C) – they are best not left in unheated rooms overnight. The one most often seen in florists' windows is *Sansevieria trifasciata* (*bound* together in threes; probably referring to the leaves); a very handsome foliage plant, with stiff, erect, sword-shaped leaves, one to four feet long, which are arranged in rosettes arising from a creeping rhizome (a fleshy root-stock such as the common Iris or Flag produces). These leaves, dark green and slightly glaucous, are armed with a stout green point and beautifully marked on both sides with transverse whitish wavy bands, and are edged with a wide, deep, green line. The flowers, greenish-white, come on stems about 2 feet tall, but are uninteresting and are frequently removed before they develop. There is a charming variety called *Laurentii* (sometimes listed as a separate species); it is like the type except that its leaf-margins are longitudinally striped golden-yellow. Propagation of this plant (Var. *Laurentii*) is only by suckers or by division; leaf cuttings always produce the type plant.

*Sansevieria trifasciata*

*S. trifasciata* is often confused with *S. thyrsiflora,* another charming foliage plant with smaller leaves and a narrow brownish-red line along the edges. The leaves (the largest: 18 inches long and 3 inches wide) are marked with transverse bands of pale green. The flowers, like those of the other kinds, are unattractive; they are white tinged with greenish-brown and come in a terminal raceme 1 to 2 feet long. The specific epithet *thyrsiflora* means having flowers in a thyrse, which is a many-flowered sort of inflorescence.

*Sansevieria hahnii*

*S. zeylanica* is the species with the popular name of Bow-string Hemp, a name generally used apparently for all the Sansevierias; though in the shops the few kinds that are on sale are known as Snake plants or Leopard Lilies. *Sansevieria* leaves contain strong, elastic, fibres, which were used in the past by native peoples in making bow-strings – hence the popular name. Many species are cultivated for the valuable fibre they yield – it is used, for instance, for mats, rope, and certain kinds of native hats. *S. zeylanica*, a native of the East Indies, has sword-shaped leaves (the largest 2 feet long and an inch thick at the base); they are dull green, with white markings and margins conspicuously red-lined; the flowers are greenish-white.

Sansevierias need a perfectly-drained sandy loamy compost and should be repotted annually, either in late spring or early summer. Keep them dry all through the winter months and give them a warm sunny place in a room. The species *S. grandis*, however, cannot be grown successfully in a living-room, for it needs a humid (jungle) atmosphere such as can be provided only in a specially-heated greenhouse. It is a magnificent plant, with enormous leaves; some are 4 feet tall and 6 inches across; they are a dull green, marked with bands of deeper green, and have red-brownish margins. This plant, a native of Tropical Africa, yields an excellent tough fibre. *S. hahnii*, on the other hand, is a favourite house plant, though a little difficult to get at times; it has short triangular-shaped leaves which come in rosettes, and are similarly marked and coloured to those of *S. trifasciata*. *Sansevieria* belong to the Lily family, *Liliaceae* and the name commemorates Raimond de Sansgrio, Prince of Sanseviero (1710–71), an Italian patron of horticulture.

*Sedum* is a genus of about 300 species. Some of the hardy succulent kinds were described in Chapter 5, page 133 and following pages. There are as many tender kinds that are amenable to pot or pan culture and make excellent house plants. They all need a winter room temperature of around 45F (7C) and benefit from being stood outside in their pots (plunged in ashes) during the summer months. A good fairly-light loamy soil suits most of them; one or two however (*Sedum lineare variegatum*, for instance) flourish more luxuriantly in a richer compost, and they all need plenty of water during hot weather and when they are making new growth. These tender succulents are readily raised from seeds; some are easily propagated by root division or by stem cuttings, depending on the habit of the plant.

*Sedum Adolphii* is a native of Mexico and is a loosely bushy plant (easy to increase by division), with erect or sprawling branches about 12 inches in length – an excellent *Sedum* for a hanging-basket in a warm living-room protected from draughts. Its great attraction is its yellowish-green narrow fleshy leaves (1½ inches long) with red margins; they are flat on the upper surface and slightly rounded beneath. The flowers are white, star-shaped, about ¾-inch wide and come in compact clusters during the early spring. This species prospers well in a light sandy leafy soil.

*S. allantoides* (*sausage-shaped*; referring to the leaves), is also from Mexico and found growing in mountainous regions (6000 feet above sea-level). It is another shrubby Sedum; branching from the base, the stems being erect and crowded with fat juicy-looking very attractive leaves. They are delightfully glaucous, cylindrical and obtuse (thick, not pointed at the tip) $\frac{3}{4}$ to an inch long. The individual flowers, $\frac{1}{2}$-inch wide, come in loose clusters, 5 inches long and 3 inches across. The colour is greenish-white. The plant blooms in July and needs plenty of water throughout the summer. It is one of those Sedums that benefit enormously from being stood out in the garden during hot weather. *S. pachyphyllum* is very similar but has red-tipped leaves (of great beauty) and yellow flowers in April.

*S. dendroideum* (tree-like) is a shrubby plant but not tree-like as regards height – it seldom goes above two feet. Perhaps the leaves clustered at the ends of the shoots give it a miniature tree-like appearance. The leaves, $1\frac{3}{4}$ inches long, are fleshy, round, and flat or disc-shaped (orbicular), with rounded tips and white wax-like margins, which later turn red in colour. The flowers are yellow and come in big clusters during the summer. This species, found in Mexico, resembles *S. confusum,* which is reasonably hardy in warm gardens. In the latter plant, however, the leaves are smaller and the inflorescence, also smaller, is more compact. The origin of the plant is unknown.

*S. lineare variegatum* (*long, narrow; variegated*) is found in China and Japan and is a species of loosely-tufted habit, with reddish decumbent stems (lying along the ground), which often root where they grow. (It is an easy plant to propagate.) The flower-stems are 6 inches and grow erect. Like most of these tender Sedums, it has very attractive leaves; they grow in whorls of three up the stems; they are lanceolate (spear-shaped), the longest measuring $1\frac{1}{2}$ inches; and they have attractive marginal stripes of white or cream. The flowers are star-shaped, yellow, and come in loose clusters about $1\frac{1}{2}$ inches wide.

*S. nussbaumerianum* (*Nussbaum* is German for nut-tree; *Nuss,* nut, probably refers to the shape of the fleshy 2-inch-long leaves). The stems are brownish, and in mature plants reach a height of 10 inches or so. The leaves are set wide apart on the lower part of the stem, but crowded, almost rosette-fashion, at the top – perhaps reminiscent of clusters of pea-nuts; they are yellowish-green in colour, flat on the upper surface and slightly rounded beneath. This species occurs in hot sandy regions of Vera Cruz (Mexico) facing the Gulf of Mexico.

*S. Palmeri* (in honour of Dr. E. Palmer, botanist and collector, who worked in Mexico); a low, spreading, Sedum found in the States of Coahuila and Nueva Leon in Northern Mexico. The stems, 6 to 9 inches long, are decumbent and rooting and glaucous like the leaves, which are oblongish, an inch long and $\frac{3}{4}$-inch wide, with a short tip. The flowers, $\frac{1}{4}$-inch across, are orange and come in loose, drooping clusters;

they are at their best in early summer. It is a very slow growing plant.

*S. Stahlii* (in honour of Christian Ernst Stahl, 1848–1919, professor of botany at Jena); a species from the State of Puebla in central Mexico and one of the most popular with collectors. Gardeners living in warm maritime districts have found it hardy enough to grow in a sheltered rockery; but as birds devour the leaves quickly (denuding the stems in a matter of hours apparently), it must be given some sort of protection; I recommend black cotton stretched tightly above it on sticks. This plant sheds its leaves naturally in the autumn; they root where they fall and consequently provide plenty of new young plants every year. The leaves, egg-shaped, thick, fleshy and very blunt, are ¾-inch long and turn reddish-brown in bright sunlight. They are carried on spreading stems about 6 inches long. The flowers are an attractive shade of yellow and come in terminal clusters about 2 inches across. They bloom indoors in August; outside toward the end of September.

*S. Treleasei* (named in honour of William Trelease, 1857–1945, Professor of Botany, University of Illinois); this species, from Mexico, is related to *S. Adolphii*, already described (see page 187), which has smooth stems and yellowish-green narrow leaves. *S. Treleasei* is easily distinguished by its glaucous, pruinose leaves, and its bright yellow flowers, which bloom in April. The leaves are crowded at the tips of the shoots, which become brown and woody with age. It is one of the shrubby species, easily increased by division.

Many of these Sedums resemble some of the Echeverias and Pachyphytums; on the whole the Sedums are easier to grow; most of them will thrive in an unheated room during the winter, provided they are kept dry. *Sedum,* like *Echeveria* and *Pachyphytum,* belong to the Crassula family, *Crassulaceae.*

*Sempervivum* (Family *Crassulaceae*) are all hardy plants as already mentioned (Chapter Five, page 138) but one or two are so beautiful that they deserve to be grown in pots as house plants. In addition to those described in Chapter Five, there is the lovely *Sempervivum Schlenhanii var. rubifolium* (*with red leaves*), a hardy plant that certainly deserves a pot and a sunny place on a window-sill. The type occurs from Hungary to Southern Greece and is frequently grown as a house plant. The correct name of this species is *S. marmoreum* (*marbled; mottled*); the name describes the flushed-red colouring of the surface of the leaves. In the variety *rubifolium* the leaves are wholly red; the plant needs a light sandy soil (2 parts coarse sand to one part sifted leafmould is recommended) and no water should be given during the winter months.

*Senecio* (Family *Compositae*) is probably the largest genus in the vegetable kingdom. There are about 1,300 different species which are found in all parts of the world.[1] Most of the succulent kinds, however, occur in South Africa and many of these are now described under the genus *Kleinia* (see pages 173 to 175). Most nurseries offer *Senecio stapeliiformis* and its varieties, and *S. scaposus,* natives of South Africa.

*S. scaposus* (*with scapes* – which are leafless flower-stalks) is an attractive shrubby succulent for a pot. It is a branched species ultimately reaching a height of about 12 inches. It has fleshy, blunt, almost cylindrical leaves (2 to 3 inches long), which are crowded at the tips of the shoots; these leaves are white-felted, cobwebby at first, then later become smooth and green. The small daisy-like flowers are yellow and are borne in a cluster of three at the end of a 12-inch stalk. But the leaves are far more attractive. This *Senecio* must be kept reasonably dry all through the winter months.

*Kleinia stapeliiformis*

*S. stapeliiformis* (*Stapelia-shaped;* probably referring to the stems) is perhaps more frequently described under the specific name of

[1] *Senecio* is known as a cosmopolitan genus.

*Kleinia stapeliiformis.* As this plant forms underground horizontal stems it is best grown in a fairly wide-topped pan where it will have plenty of room to expand. It sends up erect stems 8 inches tall, 4 to 7 angled, and ¾-inch thick. Each angle (or ridge of the stem) bears tiny, awl-shaped (sharp, pointed) leaves ¼-inch long which as they age become spine-like. The grooves, between the ridges, are grey-green and lined with dark green. The flower-heads (scarlet) are 1½ inches wide and carried singly on erect stalks about 6 inches long. The blooming season is early summer. In late summer, when the flowers have faded, the plant should be rested and watered only very occasionally: just keep the soil from drying out completely.

The variety *S. stapeliiformis var. minor* (sometimes listed as *var. Gregori*) has thinner, rather less fleshy, stems. They are five-angled, but the ridges are not so prominent. The flowers are scarlet, similar to those of the type. The popular name of this variety is Peppermint Stick.

These succulent Senecios need a perfectly-drained light loamy soil and are readily propagated by cuttings or division. During the winter they should be kept in a room with a temperature around 45F (7C). The generic name is from the Latin *senex,* old, aged, an old person (a name used by the naturalist Pliny – AD 23–79); it refers to the white hair-like pappus (downy or hairy part of the faded flowers).

*Stapelia* is a genus of about 90 species of succulent plants. Only a few, however, are found in collections. Catalogues list usually not more than three or four. The common name is Carrion Flower – many are evil-smelling – and the family is *Asclepiadaceae.* The botanist William Rhind writing about the plants in 1857 said they were introduced into England about the end of the 18th century. 'Some of the species,' he wrote 'are used as articles of food by the native Hottentots and by the Dutch settlers at the Cape, in the form of a pickle.' Stapelias inhabit dry regions in Tropical and South Africa and, according to some botanists, East India as well. Not *all* the flowers are evil-smelling but many are: those of *Stapelia Leendertziae* positively stink. In fine weather the flowers are pollinated by blowflies attracted by the smell of what they obviously thought was rotting meat or fish. Under cultivation, say in a greenhouse, Stapelias are best not raised from seed, since they hybridise readily and consequently the seedlings produced would not be of pure strain. It is much better to propagate the plants by cuttings or division. Rhind in his article says: 'Stapelias are readily propagated by cuttings. These should be laid to dry in the stove (hothouse) till they begin to shrivel, and if planted in this state in pots they will root in a very short time. If planted immediately on separation from the stem, and when full of juice, they are very apt to rot.' (The method is well known, of course, and has already been described in these pages.) It is important to remember that the cuttings require a temperature around 55F (13C). And if it can be kept up to 60F (16C) or more they will root at any time of the year.

*Stapelia variegata*

*Stapelia variegata* (*irregularly-coloured; variegated*) is by far the most popular of the species grown; and there are more than 80 named forms, all so variable and inconstant that they can seldom if ever be reproduced true to type. The species is a native of Cape Province and has grey-green stems (mottled with purple – often turning reddish in bright sunlight). The stems, leafless and angled, like those of the other species, vary from 2 to 6 inches in length and are covered with irregular protuberances (wart-like swellings), which bear sharp spines. The plant forms branches and spreads rather untidily; the flowers are fleshy, star-shaped, 2 to 3 inches in diameter, pale yellow, and blotched with dark purple.

*S. Desmetiana* (commemorating M. de Smet, nurseryman of Ghent, Belgium), from Cape Province and regions of South East Africa, a species with very striking flowers; they are large, with the five petal-like lobes reflexed and wrinkled, pale to dark purple in colour and with yellow lines; the margins of the lobes and the centre of the flower bear long purplish-white hairs. This is one of the most decorative of the Stapelias and makes a fine house plant. The stems are thick and velvety, about 12 inches tall, a pleasing shade of green; the angles are much compressed and the teeth quite inconspicuous.

*S. gigantea* (*unusually large*; referring to the flowers), a native of Natal, Transvaal, South and North Rhodesia. It is certainly the most arresting of all the Stapelias known to collectors and botanists. Its flowers measure 14 to 16 inches in diameter when fully open; the pointed lobes (petal-like organs) are pale yellow and marked with fine red transverse lines and have long white hairs at the margins. The stems are fleshy, pale green, velvety-looking, and about 8 inches tall on mature plants; the angles are compressed and have small green teeth on the ridges.

*S. grandiflora* (*large-flowered*) but the flowers are nowhere near as large as those of *S. gigantea*: they are 6 inches wide, measuring across from tip to tip of the lobes, which are brownish-purple in colour and edged with hairs. The stems, up to 12 inches in height, have a dense covering of soft hairs, which give them a charming velvety appearance; the angles are compressed and notched. This *Stapelia* (another species from Cape Province) makes a most attractive house plant.

*S. Leendertziae*, mentioned above, I have never yet seen in any private collection; it has unusual flowers for the genus, these being bell-shaped, about 3 inches long and 3 to 4 inches wide at the mouth; they are purple-black in colour and unfortunately smell of rotting fish. The plant is singularly attractive when in full bloom but doubtless not many people would want to grow it as a house plant. It is named in honour of Miss Reins Leendertz (Mrs. Pott), botanical assistant at Pretoria.

Stapelias are among the more intractable succulents grown indoors and indeed have been called specialists' plants. However, many amateurs have succeeded with them, probably because they have carefully studied their likes and dislikes. In nature these plants grow in the shade of shrubs, and consequently in a living-room, say on a window-sill facing due south, should be protected from the glaring summer sun. And they must never be overwatered, or they will begin to rot off and may eventually perish. As they are shallow-rooting plants, they do best in rather shallow pans and should be given a well-drained porous compost – put plenty of crocks at the bottom of the pan and on top a mixture of sandy loam, powdered peat or leaf-mould, coarse sand and broken brick. The growing season is from spring to summer, when the plants need most water; in winter they should be kept fairly dry (though never desert dry) and given a sunny place in a greenhouse or a room with a temperature around 50F (10C). The flowering period is in the autumn; the buds large and globular, open with a pop and usually very quickly when the room temperature is above 60F (16C). Some specialists advocate repotting every second year; others state that pot-bound Stapelias flower best. However, when the plants cease to make normal healthy growth they must be repotted, fresh soil given to them and old worn-out stems cut back or removed completely. Stapelias are perhaps the showiest of all the flowering succulents we grow indoors. The plants have been much admired by botanists ever since the time of the great Linnaeus (1707–1778); and it was he who named the genus after the Dutch physician Johannes Bodaeus van Stapel, who died in 1631.

*Tradescantia* – the Spiderworts – are as common in collections of house plants as Stapelias are rare. Practically everybody grows *Tradescantia zebrina* (*striped with different colours*) popularly known as the Wandering Jew; it has now been renamed *Zebrina pendula* but is still sold in most florists' as Tradescantia. It makes an excellent foil plant to most of the cacti and succulents we grow: 3 or 4 could be set at the front of a largish pan and allowed to trail over the side; behind them, in the centre of the pan any of the shallow-rooting succulents could be grown – I suggest *Stapelia variegata*, with its magnificent yellow and dark purple flowers. These plants could, of course, be similarly grown in a hanging-basket. The only *Tradescantia* listed in current catalogues is *T. navicularis* (*boat-shaped*; referring to the leaves). It is a native of Peru – Tradescantias are found in North and Tropical America – and if kept in a warm room or a frost-proof greenhouse *T. navicularis* will often bloom during the winter; its normal flowering season is summer. It is a low-growing, spreading plant, with ovalish fleshy, grey-green leaves, $\frac{3}{4}$-inch long, keeled or boat-shaped and pointed at the tip. They are fringed with hairs, dotted beneath and crowded together. The stems are flexuose (serpentine), and the flowers, an inch wide, are bright rose, 3-petalled, and usually at their best during the summer months.

*T. Crassula* is more difficult to get but is sometimes offered by florists. It has fleshy branching stems, 18 inches long, carrying 4-inch-long oblong leaves, with hairy margins. The flowers are white ($\frac{1}{2}$-inch wide) and come usually in terminal clusters. This species, from Brazil, blooms in July, and makes a good companion for the other. Both plants need a leafy loamy soil (2 parts garden loam to one part sifted leafmould and a sprinkling of coarse sand); and they are readily increased by cuttings inserted in a light sandy soil in gentle heat. The room temperature of these Tradescantias should not fall below 50F (10C). The genus, which belongs to the *Commelinaceae* family, was named in honour of John Tradescant, gardener to King Charles I of England.

*Yucca* belong to the Lily family, *Liliaceae* and are tall big plants, mostly grown outside in semi-tropical countries. Some, however, are reasonably hardy and one or two of these have already been mentioned: see Chapter Five, page 141. Only a few are grown in pots; they remain quite dwarf when so cultivated, but when transferred to the garden (in warm places) soon begin to grow tall. The popular name is Adam's Needle, though as a rule it is used only for the species *Yucca filamentosa* from the South Eastern United States. The generic name is from *yuca*, the Carib (Caribbean) name for the Manihot, erroneously used – the Manihot includes the edible roots of the Cassava and also rubber-producing plants. Yuccas are natives of the Southern United States, Mexico and Central America.

*Yucca aloifolia* (*with Aloe-like leaves*) comes from the West Indies and the South Eastern United States. It has produced several varieties, all of which are singularly attractive plants and more widely grown than the type itself. This, however, is very successful in a greenhouse border and when mature reaches a height of 10 feet or more. The stem is slender; the leaves, spine-tipped and toothed, are glaucous-green, about 18 inches long and one inch wide. The flowers, which come on a long panicle, are creamy-white, tinged with purple at the base. The favourite variety for a pot is *Y. aloifolia Quadricolor* (*four-coloured*). It grows remarkably slowly and can be left for years in the same pot. The leaves have a yellow or white band down the centre, and the lower half is tinged wine-red. The tips are sometimes similarly coloured. In the variety *Variegata* the leaves have simply whitish stripes. *Var. tricolor* has a yellow or white band down the middle; and *Var. draconis* has brighter green leaves than the type. They all make most attractive pot plants. They need a leafy loamy soil (equal parts of loam, sifted leafmould or peat and coarse sand), which must be kept moist during the spring and summer months. Drier conditions are best during the winter and a moderately warm room is suitable. Keep the plants, when possible, on a sunny window-sill.

Yuccas are easily propagated by cutting up the fleshy roots into 2-inch pieces and then potting them up in sand in gentle heat. Seed may also be sown (in a heated greenhouse) and can usually be obtained from specialist seedsmen.

*Y. filamentosa var. variegata* is another Yucca I have seen growing in pots. Its leaves, edged with curly threads, are margined and striped with yellow. It is easily raised from root cuttings and in a couple of years makes a very fine foliage plant. The type *Y. filamentosa* (*furnished with filaments or threads*; referring to the leaves) has stiff spreading leaves, slightly glaucous with numerous marginal white curly threads. The flowers are pendulous on a tall stem and yellowish-white in colour. The flowering season of plants grown outdoors is late summer.

Another species, also raised from root cuttings, and sometimes grown in a pot is *Y. baccata* (*berry-like; having fruits with a pulpy texture*); it has stiff spine-tipped leaves, rough to the touch, with margins set with coarse thread. The flowers, when they appear, are white, 3 inches long, and are carried in erect dense panicles. The fruits are edible and in America used to be dried and eaten by the native Indians during the winter. The plant occurs in Southern California and some of the adjoining States. *Y. recurvifolia var. marginata*, with leaves bordered with yellow, is also grown in pots indoors and propagated by root-cuttings – it is said to be among the hardiest of all the Yuccas in cultivation.

You may never see these pot-grown Yuccas in flower but they all make magnificent foliage plants. When the old leaves die they should be removed at once; in the garden they usually fall naturally.

Yuccas are the last plants listed in the catalogues of cacti and succulents I have at hand. Many more described in botanical dictionaries, magazines and books – actually hundreds of them. But the vast majority are difficult to get nowadays from nurseries and florists.

It is possible, of course, to see these rarer plants in botanical collections where, grown under ideal conditions and tended by skilled gardeners they prosper so well; some in fact make finer plants than they do in the wild. Furthermore, we often get good ideas on arranging the plants so that they are seen to best advantage.

Some, especially the biggest, the most wide-spreading, are always difficult to find a suitable place for in an ordinary-sized living-room.

The very rare *Cissus Juttae*, a succulent Vine, a non-climber though, from South West Africa, is perhaps suitable only for a conservatory or a greenhouse; it certainly looks out of place in a room. But I once saw a fine specimen standing in its pot in a largish hall, in a house which had central heating. (The plant needs a winter temperature round about 55F (13C). It was about 4 feet tall, with fleshy barrel-shaped stems – these store water during the dry season. (*C. Juttae* has very short branches, which produce 6-inch-long glossy green leaves and small flowers, and finally red berries). It was from berries taken away from Africa that this particular specimen was raised. This *Cissus* is an interesting succulent to grow in a pot but not outstandingly

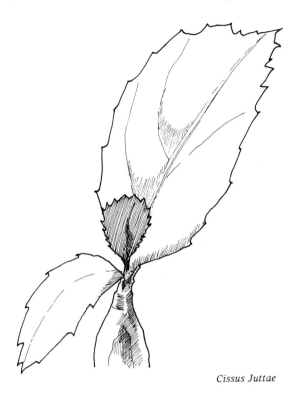

*Cissus Juttae*

attractive – many collectors call it a monstrosity. Mature plants are the most arresting; these have fat turnipy stems covered with a yellowish-green skin which peels off in papery strips. One can say of it at least that it is a plant that nobody passes by without a comment.

The plant was grown in a large flower-pot – a 14-inch size, known as a 'two' – which was stood in a highly-polished brass container. In my opinion terracotta or some sort of dull stone would have been more suitable. The glinting metal was too showy and conspicuous for the dull turnipy-looking stems of the plant; it needed, I think, a corresponding dull or matt-surfaced container. And there are plenty of them; you can choose wood, reconditioned-stone, plastic and other synthetic substances which are both unpolished and subdued in colour. Choice of a container in which to stand a pot plant needs careful consideration, for the wrong sort can detract quite considerably from the beauty of the plant. Polished brass is probably all right for a dwarf Azalea covered with masses of vivid scarlet or purple blossom.

A hall, if it is roomy enough, is the best place for the largest cacti and succulents; some of the tender species of *Agave* (see page 123) are ideal: there is *Agave parviflora*, with 4-inch-long leaves lined with white on the upper surface, which makes a bright, cheery foliage-plant for quite a small hall. Stand the pot in a globular crystal bowl in a corner. In a big hall group three together in a triangle.

*Agave stricta*, with leaves 14 inches long and $\frac{1}{2}$-inch wide, green with grey lines and finely toothed, may even bloom in time (and it doesn't die afterwards as do many of the Agaves – see page 123); the flowers, greenish-white, are produced on very long stems. This Agave, by the way, is often used for decorating a porch – one on each side of the door. The plants should be stood in wooden tubs and given some protection during severe frosty weather if left permanently in the porch.

*Agave geminiflora* is another species suitable for a hall; it has fine rush-like leaves (a very graceful-looking plant) and will live for years in a good-sized pot.

*Yucca aloifolia* (page 195) rather resembles it in shape and the variety tinted with pink at the base of the leaves (*Var. Quadricolor*) looks wonderfully decorative in a small hall – it needs no companion plants.

If you like egregious shapes, have one or two pots of *Opuntia* or *Cereus* – many are reminiscent of pieces of contemporary sculpture. The low spreading kinds of Opuntias are usually small and compact enough for limited spaces. *Opuntia microdasys Var. rufida* (page 67), with ovalish green pads and red-brown tufts of glochids makes a charming ornament; it is frequently offered for room decoration in coloured glass containers – blue, red, green.

*Cereus peruvianus* (page 39) is a tall columnar prickly cactus suitable for a big hall. As it grows taller and bigger it will, of course, need repotting and the soil renewing or enriching. One way of displaying it to advantage in a large hall is to stand it near the staircase, so that the tall angular stem can soar up against the banisters. If it is a central staircase another tall plant may be stood on the other side for the sake of symmetry; the Old Man Cactus (*Cephalocereus senilis* – page 38) would be an excellent choice.

The modern dining-room is often a dining-room-cum-lounge or -living-room. And here as a rule is accommodated the main collection of plants.

Such a room is fairly spacious and usually there are plenty of shelves; and for the house plant enthusiast what we might call a collective container (designed to hold a dozen or so smallish pots or just the plants themselves); and there is often a special low narrow table as well, about 9 inches high, standing near a sunny window. The displaying of hanging-baskets, however, poses something of a problem; the wisest thing to do is to fix up special brackets on the wall for them.

Before choosing cacti and succulents for our rooms, we must first consider the prevailing temperature; if it can be controlled, as it can by central heating, all well and good; but if the temperature drops at night or varies considerably, then we should choose only the hardiest plants.

The Christmas Cactus (page 34), although among the toughest kinds, needs a really warm temperature as it comes into bud; ungrafted specimens, with their hanging stems, are ideal for baskets. But they must have some sort of covering over them if the room gets very cold at night.

On a low narrow table by the window – sometimes called a plant table – a dozen or more small pots can be stood, or twice that number if they are small enough and are arranged in a double row. Naturally one chooses one's favourite plants. For my part I would have those that were sure to come into flower at some time of the year; though I would prefer those that bloomed in mid-winter. (The reader will find a good selection in the pages of this book).

The long moulded stone trough, mostly a neutral grey, has rightly come in for a lot of praise from indoor gardeners; for many choice tender things can be grown in it; and its great advantage is that it can be easily moved to a warm place on cold winter nights – away from the window, where it is usually kept – and perhaps put on a table near a stove. Such a receptacle is ideal for those wonderfully fascinating Mimicry plants.[1]

Bedrooms and bathrooms can scarcely be said to be lived in, consequently pot-plants may seem to be superfluous there. However, for those people who like to spend long periods in bed – or unfortunately have to – a variety of pot-grown cacti and succulents can be very agreeable to look at. And the shape and texture of many of these plants often have more appeal and are of more lasting interest than the flowers, which frequently, when they do appear, are evanescent or open only at night.

*Echeveria pulvinata*, a silvery-white velvety-looking succulent (page 161) is a plant which one can apparently look at all day without getting tired of it. Perhaps its soft velvety appearance has a soothing effect on some people. It likes a warm dry atmosphere, especially

[1] More common than the stone trough is the ordinary long narrow wooden box – which many people can make themselves.

during the winter months. One elderly lady who spent a lot of time in bed chose the patriarchial *Cephalocereus senilis*, a tall specimen with an astonishing amount of untidy grey hair – it was her favourite plant, she said, and she found it good company.

Bathrooms often have plenty of shelves but as they are filled with toilet articles we can't very well use them for pot plants. But we can fix up one or two brackets and from them hang special wire containers (if baskets are thought too large); these should be lined with moss and in them stood single pots of plants like the Christmas Cactus, *Tradescantia navicularis* (page 194) and some of the *Rhipsalis* (page 115). These have pendant stems and are very suitable and graceful plants for hanging from brackets. Furthermore, they are easily sprayed and perhaps the drips won't matter much on the bathroom floor. The moss lining should be sprayed regularly to keep it fresh and green. And while on the subject of spraying I should say that the most suitable place for this operation, apart from the kitchen sink, is the bathroom. Plants should be brought in here and stood in the bath and left there till the surplus water has drained away and the pots themselves are dry.

The modern 'home extension' (built of glass and wood or steel) is used chiefly as a place to relax in, where we can read and talk and perhaps enjoy a little solitude; it also makes an excellent garden room (a sort of miniature conservatory) where we can grow, amongst other things, our favourite cacti and succulents, which we can sit and look at and admire for as long as we like. And it is possible to prepare a bed or border containing a good depth of soil against the outside of one of the warmest walls, in which to grow a permanent collection of these plants.